The Deer on a Bicycle

Also by Patrick McManus

A Fine and Pleasant Misery, 1978

Kid Camping from AAA!!! to Zip, 1979

They Shoot Canoes, Don't They?, 1981

Never Sniff a Gift Fish, 1983

The Grasshopper Trap, 1985

Rubber Legs and White Tail-Hairs, 1987

The Night the Bear Ate Goombaw, 1989

Whatchagot Stew:
A Memoir of an Idaho Childhood with Recipes, 1989

Real Ponies Don't Go Oink!, 1991

The Good Samaritan Strikes Again, 1992

How I Got This Way, 1994

Never Cry "Arp!" and Other Great Adventures, 1996

Into the Twilight Endlessly Grousing, 1997

The Deer
on a Bicycle:
Excursions into the Writing of Humor

by

Patrick McManus

EWU
P·R·E·S·S

EASTERN WASHINGTON UNIVERSITY PRESS

SPOKANE, WASHINGTON

Acknowledgments

"The Boy" and "Into the Twilight, Endlessly Grousing" from INTO THE TWI-LIGHT, ENDLESSLY GROUSING by Patrick F. McManus. Copyright © 1997 by Patrick F. McManus. Reprinted by permission of Simon & Schuster, Inc.

"A Good Deed Goes Wrong" from REAL PONIES DON'T GO OINK by Patrick F. McManus Copyright © 1991 by Patrick F. McManus.

"Sequences" and "The Night the Bear Ate Goombaw" from THE NIGHT THE BEAR ATE GOOMBAW by Patrick F. McManus Copyright © 1989 by Patrick F. McManus.

"Muldoon in Love" from RUBBER LEGS AND WHITE TAIL-HAIRS by Patrick F. McManus Copyright © 1987 by Patrick F. McManus.

"Mean Tents" from THE GRASSHOPPER TRAP by Patrick F. McManus Copyright © 1985 by Patrick F. McManus.

"The Big Trip" and "The Two-Wheeled ATV" from A FINE AND PLEASANT MISERY by Patrick F. McManus Copyright © 1978 by Patrick F. McManus. Reprinted by arrangement with Henry Holt and Company and Patrick F. McManus.

Copyright © 2000 Patrick F. McManus

Manufactured in the United States of America

Library of Congress Cataloging-in-Publication Data
McManus, Patrick F.
        The Deer on a bicycle: excursions into the writing of humor / by
Patrick F. McManus
p. cm.
ISBN 0-910055-62-9 (pbk.)–ISBN 0-910055-63-7 (hbk.)
        1. Wit and humor–Authorship. I. Title
PN 6149.A88 M36 2000
808.7–dc21   99-089160

Book and cover design by Scott Poole, Joelean Copeland and Cynthia Dukich

For Darlene

Table of Contents

Stories with Commentaries:

Preface

As with all my undertakings, I thought this endeavor would be a much simpler project than it turned out to be. A few years ago, my wife Darlene, and I established an endowment with the Eastern Washington University Foundation to provide scholarships for creative writing and journalism students. Establishing an endowment was rather presumptuous on our part, even irrational, because we aren't exactly members of the philanthropic class. Still, we felt we should give something back to Eastern, however modest, for the twenty-three years this excellent institution put up with me as a professor (I always thought of myself as something of an impostor in the grove of academe, but I was never found out as far as I know). So D. and I came up with a plan whereby I would give writing workshops around the Pacific Northwest and the enrollment money would go into the endowment. The plan worked nicely, until after a couple of years or so, when I began to run out of both the time and energy required to continue the workshops. That's when I came up with my simple idea. I would organize my workshop notes into a small book to be published by the EWU Press, and all the proceeds could then be divided up between the Press and the Endowment. Years later, this is the result. Or at least a result.

I have no idea whether this book will help anyone to become a humor writer, or any other kind of writer for that matter. But perhaps it will at least offer encouragement in the sense of readers saying to themselves, "He can do it, I surely can!" I think that during the years I taught writing at EWU, my students took just such encouragement from me, and many of them went on to become successful and even famous writers. So they have me to thank for it. Maybe you will too.

In order to save myself undue thought on matters of organization, I have employed the same system of order for this book that I once used as a professor: chaos. To help readers find their way through the chaos, however, I have created Newton, who asks questions randomly about various topics as we go along, much as did the participants in my workshops. I reply with equal randomness, and occasionally with wild abandon. The opinions and bits of advice offered here, along with speculation, half-truths, reflections, aimless meanderings, and vague rumors, are derived from my thirty years and more of trying to extract a laugh or at least a smile from my readers, not all that easy to do in some of these harrowing times. I have tried to be as honest in my answers to Newton's questions as I know how to be, which perhaps isn't saying too much, but it is the best you can hope for. In addition, I have included several stories from among the hundreds I've published over the years. Following each story is a commentary in which I discuss how the story came about, various problems, and other matters involved in the writing of it. The stories that are truly brilliant are all the more so in their absence. No, the stories included here were selected because they illustrate various aspects of humor writing that I wish to discuss. So there.

No one will become a humor writer because he or she reads this book or any other book. People become humor writers because they can't help themselves. It is in their nature. For everyone else? Well, think of it this way: The money you spend buying this book may help sustain some students on their way to writing the next Great American Novel. Or maybe not. But at least you helped give them a shot. 🚲

Introduction

My Life and Weird Times, or How I Became a Writer of Humor

One of my many theories about writing and humor is that both ultimately arise out of the life, character and personality of the writer. Because there is not much I wish to reveal about either my character or personality, I will tell you something about my life and how I got into this occupation of humor writing.

I was born in an old farmhouse three miles north of Sandpoint, Idaho, on August 24, 1933. There is some question about the exact date of my birth, because my father got the attending doctor drunk, and the doctor mistakenly wrote in August 25, instead of August 24, as the date on my birth certificate. That is according to my mother, she and I being the only sober ones in the house at the time. I have been rather pleased with the mistake ever since I first heard about it. Confusion is the natural environment of a humor writer, and it is best to get introduced to it as early as possible.

My father died a few years after I was born, and I have only sparse memories of him. My mother taught school, usually all eight grades in little one-room structures situated in remote mountain valleys of North Idaho. The schools were surrounded by beautiful forests and mountains and streams, and a tedium so vast and dense as to be almost impenetrable! There were no movies, television, radio, magazines, newspapers, mail or malls. There were, however, books, to which I was driven not so much by a desire to learn but as a means of escape from the all-pervading boredom.

Even though my mother was a teacher, I taught myself to read. Mom had devised a torture with which she tormented not only me but her other pupils as well. Each day after the noon recess, she would read aloud to us for exactly fifteen minutes. Somehow she managed to end each reading right at a climactic moment. We would beg her to continue, but she would only chuckle evilly and order us back to work.

The time came when I could stand this abuse no longer. One day I grabbed a third-grade text, climbed up on my bed and vowed not to leave it until I had learned to read. Having somehow absorbed phonics while taking up space in the classroom, I randomly selected a story and began sounding my way through it. I sounded my way through once, without acquiring the slightest idea of what the story was about. My third or fourth time through it, the content of the story slowly began to emerge, as if from a mist. By the end of the day, I could read the story perfectly. It was about peanuts. I was surprised to learn that peanuts grow under the ground like potatoes, instead of on top of the ground like peas. Otherwise, the story was the most boring thing I've ever read in my life. By the time I completed second grade, I had become an insatiable reader, perhaps the single quality all writers have in common.

We eventually moved back to Sandpoint, where my mother taught in town and I attended a normal grade school, where I did poorly in most subjects and excelled in nothing, except possibly my hatred of school. Actually, it wasn't so much school I hated but its confinement and regimentation. Art was the only subject I cared about, and I drew and painted constantly all the way through high school. The *Saturday Evening Post* covers by Norman Rockwell served as my chief inspiration and mode of instruction. The peak achievement of my artistic career was the selection of a painting of mine to be hung in the Sandpoint Elks Club. It dustily adorned a wall of the club for decades, until an Elk official, no doubt a closet art critic, had it removed and disposed of. It is just as well.

As a freshman art major at Washington State University (then college), I soon discovered that the Fine Arts faculty and I were incompatible, and it quickly became apparent we would separate on grounds of irreconcilable differences. Difficult as it is to believe, the art faculty actually preferred the work of some guy named Picasso over the *Saturday Evening Post* covers of Norman Rockwell. There's no accounting for artistic taste, particularly among art professors.

At the same time, I developed a serious interest in English Composition—academic survival! Four weeks into the first semester, I had already accumulated as many F's on my weekly essays. Inspired by desperation, I devoted an enormous amount of time to writing my next essay, probably almost an hour. Another F! This was getting serious. I now took the extreme measure of actually opening my composition text and studying it and even consulted my dictionary from time to time. Another F! I was nearly halfway through the semester and had acquired a perfect grade-point average—.oo!

I bore down on my next essay with a diligence and concentration previously unknown to me in any academic subject. The effort paid off. A D-minus! I had made a major breakthrough. The following essay returned with a whole D. And then came a C, followed by a C-plus. Soon my days and nights and weekends were consumed with the writing of essays.

My professor even began to scribble little notes of friendly encouragement on the tops of my papers. I pushed onward. Finally, on the next-to-last week of the semester, my essay came back with an A! There was only one essay remaining, and it was the biggie for the course. It could make or break you. I selected a topic I cared passionately about and poured everything I had into it. When the prof handed back the essays on the final day of class, I peeked inside the folded paper. There, in large, blazing red at the top of the title sheet was—an A-plus! And under the A-plus was a nice note from the professor, at the end of which he mentioned that he had recommended me for Honors English the following semester. In fifteen weeks I had gone from F's to Honors English. Not too bad. What was that A-plus essay? Why, it was an appreciation of the *Saturday Evening Post* covers of Norman Rockwell! Scarcely had I learned what an irony was, than I had committed one.

Because I had invested so much time and effort in learning to write, I decided I might just as well keep going and become a writer. Besides, the life of the writer seemed the perfect one for me. You could get into it for practically nothing, which was what I had at the time: a typewriter, paper, envelopes and postage stamps, the ultimate in low overhead. As with any sophomoric writer, my goal was to become rich and famous, but I would have been well satisfied to earn a modest living in obscurity, if I could do so by writing. To my fresh, uncluttered mind, writing seemed to offer an escape from actual work, for which I had shown little aptitude and even less enthusiasm, as various of my former employers would vigorously attest.

Throughout my undergraduate years, I worked feverishly at becoming a writer, the horrifying prospect of an actual job looming ever closer. I took every writing course offered at WSU, wrote for the campus newspaper and occasionally for the school literary magazine, in which was published my first piece of fiction, "The Lady Who Kept Things."

Written in a creative writing class, the story is about a daffy housewife who can't bear to discard anything: string, foil, newspapers, table scraps, etc. She teeters on the brink of insanity, and for some reason I've forgotten, her husband decides to nudge her over the edge. He first poisons her little dog, thinking the loss of the pet will do the dastardly deed. But she has the dog stuffed and keeps it posed rigidly in front of the fireplace. The husband poisons her cat. Same result. He poisons her goldfish, which as I recall, she has pickled in their own bowl, probably with lead shot in their bellies to keep them upright. And so on. Finally, when the husband has exhausted his wife's supply of pets, he decides as a last resort that the loss of her husband will tip the wretched woman over the brink. Oddly, she takes the news of his departure rather well. She even offers him a last serving of his favorite soup. Stupidly, the husband accepts. As the dose of arsenic begins to take effect on him, he notices through blurring vision that his wife is emptying out the freezer. The final line of the story is, "It was a very large freezer."

Academically, I wasn't doing all that well as a college sophomore, except for English. Nevertheless, it came as a bit of a shock to receive a note from the dean of the College of Arts and Letters saying he wished to see me. The dean, a former Rhodes Scholar, clearly was a person possessed of a serious attitude toward academic pursuits. His note could only mean bad news for me. I wasn't sure whether to gather up my meager belongings before I went to see him, or afterwards, when I might not be allowed on campus long enough to pack. When I entered his office, the dean glanced up at me sternly, a faculty countenance with which I was not unfamiliar.

"Oh, it's you, McManus," he said, brightening. "I just wanted to tell you I enjoyed very much that little story of yours in the literary magazine about the lady who kept things. Quite good! Excellent, in fact!"

I'm unsure what field of scholarship the dean pursued, but probably not literary criticism. Nevertheless, the dean's nugget of praise has remained in my psychic poke for forty years and more, and from time to time I take it out and bask in its healing glow. Never ignore or forget any bit of praise for your writing, deserved or not. Praise possesses excellent restorative properties, particularly for the writer of humor.

As a final project for the term, the creative writing prof assigned us a paper in which we were to reveal our thought processes, if any, employed in the creation of one of our stories, the paper to be read aloud to the class. I reported on "The Lady Who Kept Things." The report, my first venture into humor, sent the class into a paroxysm of mirth, a response my fellow creative writers usually reserved for somber and serious works by their classmates. It was wonderful! The professor laughed so hard he had to take off his glasses to wipe away tears. Surely, I thought, I will finally get an A on a paper for this class. The paper came back with a B on it. I stormed into the prof's office and complained about the B. "That paper had everybody in stitches, including yourself," I told him.

"Yes, McManus," he replied, "it was a very funny paper, very funny indeed. But this is a class in the writing of serious literature. And you have to admit, that paper of yours wasn't serious."

What could I say?

So there it was, the cruel reality with which nearly all writers of humor must come to grips: the doors of literature are closed to them. My creative writing professor taught me that lesson early on. I didn't write another humor piece for fifteen years, and then, only on a whim.

While still in college, I developed an interest in journalism and was hired as a stringer, or correspondent, for the *Lewiston* (Idaho) *Morning Tribune*. There I had the good fortune to receive occasional tutelage from one of the finest newspaper editors in the country, Bill Johnston, whose editorials in his small newspaper had won him a national reputation. In occasional coffee sessions at a Lewiston café, Bill imparted to me a greater sense of journalism than any book I'd ever read or class I'd ever taken.

I'm quite sure it was a recommendation from Bill Johnston that landed me my first job after college, as a reporter on the *Daily Olympian* in the state capital, Olympia, Washington. The paper was small but the staff good, and the editor quickly honed my writing style down to a sharp edge, or at least to an edge. Perhaps more important, the number of stories he assigned me, to be pounded out by deadline *or else*, soon gave me a detachment in regard to my writing that has served me well ever since.

To write for publication is to expose yourself on the printed page. You alone are out there, psychically naked for all to see and comment on, often unkindly. I believe it is the inability of beginning writers to achieve at least a certain degree of detachment from their writing that defeats so many of them before they even get started. Without this distancing, any criticism of your writing will seem devastating, even incapacitating, whereas with the proper amount of detachment it will seem merely cruel and unusual punishment.

A long time ago, I gave up reading reviews of my books, even though most were favorable and some were glowing. There is always the bad one, written by some insipid idiot who wouldn't know sheer brilliance if he fell in it. Reading reviews, no matter how wonderful, is always a downer. You can read sentence after sentence of the most wonderful praise, but the reviewer, perhaps to indicate his objectivity, feels he must, near the very end of the review, insert at least one negative comment: "Even though this work is one of the three greatest novels ever written, I did feel the author made excessive use of the comma." In response, the enraged author screams, "What! How dare that fool criticize my commas?" One negative comment will burn holes in the author's psyche for years afterwards. Take my word, it is best not to read reviews.

After my brief stint at newspapering, I was next hired to edit and write for the publications department back at Washington State University, a job which gave me the opportunity to complete my master's degree in English. This in turn allowed me to land a job teaching English and Journalism at Eastern Washington University (then a state college). Teaching, much to my surprise, turned out to top the scale of hard work. Bad choice! Bad choice! But what could I do? Because I lacked a Ph.D., my future in the groves of academe promised very thin pickings. So I decided to get serious about writing. I set up a writing schedule of two hours a day, 7:00 pm—9:00 pm, seven evenings a week, and tried never to miss a single day.

The writing schedule required that I *write* for two hours each day—not do research, not read about writing, not think about writing, not make notes about what I intended to write, but actually to pound the keys for a full two hours, whether or not I had anything to write about. I hated it! But after a couple of months of sticking ruthlessly to this schedule, I experienced a peculiar psychological adjustment. Like Pavlov's dog anticipating the supper bell, but with less drooling, I began to feel a compulsive pull toward the typewriter as seven o' clock approached each night. I could barely wait to get back to whatever story or article I had been working on. Also, I noticed that my writing had become, if not easier, substantially better. Rather good phrases appeared on the page, seemingly before I had even thought of them. Sometimes it seemed as if the typewriter, my old manual Royal Standard, was doing the writing by itself. I don't believe you can succeed as a writer, at least professionally, unless writing becomes virtually compulsive for you. Otherwise, you must fall back on self-discipline, and we all know what a bore that is.

Set up a daily writing schedule. That is the best advice I can offer any aspiring writer. If nothing else, the schedule will make you think of yourself as a writer. I also have a theory that daily writing raises the subconscious to a level where it accesses the conscious and slips into it the words, phrases and ideas that appear magically on paper, seemingly before you have even thought of them. In any case, after a few months of sticking to your schedule, you should be rewarded with an astonishing improvement in your writing. If not, there's always computer programming.

After setting up my writing schedule, I suddenly began selling articles and stories to a wide variety of national magazines, something that had never occurred with my irregular bursts of writing. Checks large and small and minuscule began arriving in the mail, but no matter the size, each conveyed to me the sense that at last I had become a professional writer, namely one who gets paid for his or her writing.

I wrote my first humor piece one evening in 1968. I had not intended to write a humor piece, but after completing an article on the use of telemetry in the study of wildlife, that is, hooking up wild creatures to radio transmitters in order to spy on their nocturnal affairs, I still had an hour left to go in my writing period. Not wishing to start another factual article that evening, I decided to use up the remaining hour simply by writing some nonsense. My head still filled with the telemetry piece, it occurred to me to extend that topic into absurdity—namely that sometime in the future *all* wildlife would be hooked up with radio transmitters.

The completed piece didn't strike me as particularly funny, but my writing program had yet another rule: anything I wrote during my writing session had to be mailed out to market. So I dutifully mailed off the manuscript. One day several weeks later, an envelope arrived from *Field & Stream* magazine. It contained a check for $300, along with a small brass band, which immediately struck up a happy tune in celebration of my first sale of a humor piece.

I made some quick calculations. Recently, I'd received $750 for a factual article that required months of research. The $300 humor piece required no research and only an hour of writing time. Hmmmm, I mused. Let's see now, I write two hours a day, which means I can produce two $300-humor pieces every night, and I write seven days a week. That works out to $600 a day, $4,200 a week! I'll be rich! Rich!

Okay, so it didn't quite work out that way. But that is how I became a writer of humor. 🚲

Newton's Questions

Newton: Pat, what do you mean by "indirection" in a story?

I'm sorry you brought that one up, Newt. Let's see. Hmm.

Well, indirection is where you don't write about what you intend to write about but write about something else that in some way reveals what it was you actually wanted to write about. All clear about that?

You don't go directly at what you want to write about. Humor might almost be defined as an exercise in indirection, because you almost never come out and say what you mean straight on.

In Ernest Hemingway's *On Writing* (ed. Larry W. Phillips, Touchstone, 1999), Hem is quoted thusly: "I try always to do the thing by three-cushion shots rather than by words or direct statements. But maybe we must have direct statement too."

"Be obscure clearly," E.B. White wrote somewhere.

I somehow drifted into indirection and obscurity by accident. I didn't know what I was doing until someone happened to mention it to me. I'm sure that all my best stories were done with at least one-cushion shots.

In my story "Into the Twilight, Endlessly Grousing," I wanted to write humorously about a warm relationship between a younger man and an older man. In a broader sense, the story is about how men tend to relate to each other as friends. They do so by indirection. So I wrote the story using indirection to show the indirection men use in expressing affection for each other. They do so by grousing at each other throughout the whole story, which also appears to be a grouse-hunting trip. If that isn't a three-cushion shot, what is?

Let's say you want to write about your Aunt Agnes as being a really neat lady. You could go straight at Aunt Agnes with your ballpoint pen, but the story probably wouldn't be very interesting. Maybe instead you could approach Agnes as being a very strict and even harsh disciplinarian, who made your life miserable. That's the way you saw her when you were a child. In the course of your story, however, events and actions reveal bit by bit that your aunt was truly a kind, caring, and amazing woman.

That, I think, is what Hemingway meant by "a three-cushion shot" and what E.B. White meant by, "Be obscure clearly." Ultimately, the reader should be able to get the point of it all.

In his novel *The Ambassadors*, Henry James uses a rather interesting double point of view. We see a scene through the mind of Lambert Strether, but we also see it objectively off to the side of Strether's head. It is as though the vision of one eye passes through Strether's mind and the vision of the other eye goes past Strether's right ear to the objective scene. Thusly can the reader compare Strether's interpretation of what he sees with the reader's interpretation of what he or she sees from the objective viewpoint. You, the reader, want to shout out, "Are you stupid or what Strether! Don't you see what is happening here?" The obscurity lies in the fact that you cannot take Strether's interpretation of events as being the correct one. Henry James, by the way, is an acquired taste. Somewhere Mark Twain wrote of his novels, "If you lay one down, it's awfully hard to pick it back up again."

Obscurity must have a purpose. I once read a creative writing student's novel in which one of the main characters simply disappears. No explanation. Duke is just suddenly gone from the novel without any clues to his disappearance.

"Whatever happened to Duke?" I asked the student. "He just suddenly disappears, and he never shows up again."

The student didn't miss a beat. "I did that on purpose to create a little mystery," he explained. Yeah, right. You don't create mystery for the sake of mystery. You don't create obscurity for the sake of obscurity.

So obscure clearly, and work on that three-cushion shot.

Newton: *Why write for magazines? Why not go straight to authoring books, which could turn out to be best-sellers and make you rich and famous right off?*

Many authors do go straight to writing books, and some do hit the big time, but let's start with this simple question: How do you get the book published in the first place? And once it is published, how does anyone know it has been published?

One good reason for doing magazine work, aside from keeping bread on the table, is that you can develop a sizable audience familiar with your writing and name, and you can do so rather quickly, if your magazine readers like what you write. A ready-made audience for a proposed book is a major enticement for publishers. It used to be said that if a first book sold five thousand copies it was a success, meaning that the publisher had broken even on the deal and thus would be interested in publishing your next book. I don't know if five thousand is still the magic number, but let's suppose it is. If you write for a publication that has, say two hundred thousand subscribers, and you have a following of readers among the two hundred thousand, there's a good chance you can sell five thousand copies to that audience alone. Magazine editors are usually very good about notifying their subscribers that one of their writers has a new book out. So that's how two hundred thousand people will learn you've just published a new book. Any established audience for your writing is better than none at all when it comes to selling a book to a publisher. Mention of an available audience in your book proposal will at least get an editor to scratch his chin and ponder whether he should publish your book. So that is why it's a good idea to write for magazines. 🚲

Newton: How do I know where to send my manuscript?

First, either buy or check out of the library a copy of *Writer's Market*. It is filled with just about every market that exists for writers, as well as lots of other good information, such as which publications are looking for humor, names of editors, rates paid, etc. Once you find a publication you might want to write for, hunt down as many copies as you can find. Study these copies thoroughly. Note the advertising. Look at the car ads in particular. If the cars in the ads are the kind that start at $50,000 and go up, the reader—and editors—probably aren't interested in an article on how to tour Europe on $25 a day. Ads can give you a pretty clear idea of the kind of reader you are dealing with in a particular magazine, or at least the kind of readers the editors think read their magazine. It's always important to remember that magazines are businesses, and advertising is both the means and purpose of their existence.

Many of the magazines listed in *Writer's Market* are not to be found in most libraries or on magazine racks at the supermarket. Because many of these magazines depend on freelancers, most are willing to send interested writers sample copies to study.

Few things offend a magazine editor more than receiving a query that makes it evident that the writer has never even bothered to look through a copy of the magazine. So study your markets.

Some freelance writers are more marketing experts than they are writers. They will write an article about vacationing in a lighthouse, for example, and then they might sell essentially the same travel section article to different newspapers without overlapping circulations—a Boston paper, a Dallas paper, a Chicago paper, and so on. The writer must tell each of the editors that he is sending out multiple submissions of the article, but the editors won't mind as long as they've been informed and there is no overlapping of circulation. That same article might also be sold to a travel magazine, with a different slant and different photos than the version sold to newspapers. It might be re-slanted to an airline magazine, or a magazine directed at retirees, like *Modern Maturity*. A friend of mine once sold an article on snowshoeing to fifteen different magazines, changing only the photos and the slant for each publication. For an airline magazine, the slant might be that snowshoeing is an interesting way for executives to get winter exercise in parks near their homes or offices. For an outdoor sports magazine, the slant might be: here's an old way to explore wilderness in the winter. And so on.

In order to make a living freelance writing, you either have to be very good at writing or very good at marketing. You had better be pretty good at both if you expect to make more than a modest income from your writing.

Notes in *Writer's Market* will tell you if the editor wants to see a query first or the completed article. Most want queries.

A good query letter can take almost as much time to write as the article itself. You need to start right off with your editorial concept, which probably won't differ much from the lead in your article. Here is essentially the same lead I used to sell my lookout story to *Sports Illustrated*.

Mr. Ray Cave
Articles Editor
Sports Illustrated
New York, NY

Dear Mr. Cave:
How about an article for SI on "Wild Life in a Room with a View?" Each June, about the time most people begin moving to the seashore, a few hundred strangely assorted Americans

head for the high mountains and great forests of the land. Their stated purpose is to help prevent forest fires. But what they really have in mind is the ultimate get-away-from-it-all, an escape into the blissful solitude of a delightful little wilderness penthouse—a U.S. Forest Service lookout station. Helping to prevent forest fires is merely the price they must pay for their room with a view. Early each September, out they come again, and from their stories one wonders if the solitude is all that blissful, the price that mere or the penthouse that delightful; there are, it seems a few trials and even some tribulations. The lookouts are besieged by lightning, wild beasts, insects, sun, fire, and worst of all, the monstrous boredom. As one forest ranger says, the work consists largely of just being there.

If that sounds like an article SI could use, I would submit it on speculation. My work has been published in Blaw, Blaw, Blaw and Blaw.

End of query.

If you check "Wild Life in a Room with a View," you will see that the query letter is almost the same as the lead on the article. It opens with the editorial concept, goes to the slant, "most people think of vacations" (SI does vacation travel articles), goes to the spread, "strangely assorted Americans" and then sets up the idea for the article—the blissful little penthouse in the wilderness turns out not to be that blissful.

Back when I was writing factual articles, I almost always researched and interviewed for humorous anecdotes, because I knew that readers always enjoyed a little humor with their facts. I also knew humorous anecdotes appealed to editors. For that reason, I always tried to reduce the anecdotes to a series of phrases in the query letter. In a query I wrote about "The One-Thousand-Dollar Television Historical Extravaganza" (editorial concept), a story about a series of half-hour historical dramas produced by a local TV station on a very tight budget, I listed some of the problems the crew had to overcome:

"—The 'soldiers' who ran away from their sewer-pipe cannon whenever they fired it—the 'Indian' wearing a digital wristwatch—the wagon train consisting of only one wagon—the art director who came up with the idea of spray painting the 'Indians' red—etc." I listed about eight or so of the anecdotes in this fashion, and I know it was the anecdotes that caught the attention of the editors and eventually sold the story. I highly recommend that writers research and interview for humorous anecdotes, and other anecdotes as well. Reduce each to a brief phrase and list them in the query. The facts in your article will inform, but the anecdotes will entertain. So you end up with an article that is both informative and entertaining. What editor could ask for more?

There is no point in submitting a query letter for a humor piece. Just send in the piece itself, because with humor everything depends on the writing. What would you say in a humor query letter anyway, "I have just written this hysterically funny story about thingamajigs?" With humor, the only thing to do is keep firing off your pieces until an editor finally breaks down and buys one. Humor is always a tough sell for any writer and particularly so for anyone who is just getting started. Always remember, the writer who succeeds is the one with staying power. 🚲

Newton: How did your first book get published, Pat?

It wasn't easy, Newton. By 1975, I had been writing comic stories for *Field & Stream* and other magazines for about six years. *Field & Stream* by itself had at least five million readers, for whom I'd become one of the more popular writers in the magazine. It seemed reasonable to me, therefore, that the book publishers would fight each other to bring out a collection of my stories. Such was not the case.

Nearly all first-time book authors run into the same chicken-egg dilemma. That is, they can't get a publisher without an agent, and they can't get an agent without a publisher. I don't have any solutions to that dilemma, but here is how I went about getting my first book, *A Fine and Pleasant Misery*, published.

I vaguely recall that I tried to interest some agents in my book, but without success. At some point, I decided to start sending my book proposal directly to publishers.

I typed up half a dozen of my published stories and clipped the illustrations from *Field & Stream* to them, just to add a bit of color and to make them more attractive. It's possible some editors rejected the stories instantly on the grounds that my decorations revealed me as either a total amateur or a total nut. I also included a cover letter emphasizing that I had already acquired a sizable audience in the magazine field and therefore had considerable name familiarity as a writer. The book had a huge audience eagerly awaiting it, I explained modestly.

I sent out the packet of stories and my cover letter to a publisher—I can't remember which one. Months passed. Finally, the manuscript returned with a nice letter of rejection. The editor said that his staff had thoroughly enjoyed the stories, but alas, "collections don't sell." That was a refrain I was to hear over and over again.

The first publisher had taken so long to return my book proposal that I figured it might be well into the next century by the time I'd sent the book to every publisher one submission at a time. So I made up three sets of the proposal and sent them out to three publishers at once. As soon as one was rejected, I'd send it out again, usually after it had been retyped or otherwise cleaned up.

After nearly two years of this process, I finally gave up. My family and I packed up and moved to Mexico for a few months. Scarcely had we settled into an apartment in Guadalajara, than I got a call from an editor at Holt, Rinehart and Winston to tell me Holt was taking the book. The next day I got a call from a famous agent, saying he would like to represent me. And the next day I got a call from an editor at Doubleday, saying her company wanted the book. I'd spent two years trying to peddle A *Fine and Pleasant Misery* without success. Then within three days I received offers from two different publishers and acquired an agent. See how it works? 🚲

Newton: *Why do you give your characters and places such odd names?*

For the most part, I try to give characters and places funny names, because these after all, are intended to be humor pieces. I hope that the names Retch Sweeney, Rancid Crabtree, Troll, Crazy Eddie, Strange, etc., will tell the reader something about the character of the person or place. "Retch" suggests this character is probably not the smartest and most sophisticated guy around. "Rancid" is not all that fond of baths. By calling my sister "Troll," I give the reader a quick indication of my relationship with her. "Strange" probably isn't the greatest dog in the world, either.

If Retch and I stop for breakfast at Gert's Gas & Grub, the reader can be pretty sure this is not a place where customers expect cloth napkins. I assume that the reader has eaten in many such places and given a clue in the name, can furnish most of the greasy details. Because of the brevity required for short humor, one must constantly look for ways to save words. Comically descriptive names for characters and places are one of mine.

Newton: Can one learn to see funny?

I don't know. Maybe "seeing funny" is a psychological aberration one is born with. As far back as I can remember, I have always seen funny. What may horrify normal people may strike me as hilarious. Here's an example:

Two friends and I were visiting a rancher in Montana. It was getting late in the day and a blizzard was blowing in. Suddenly, the rancher said, "Say, I've got this canyon I want to show you boys." With some reluctance, my friends and I piled into the rancher's old truck. When we got to the steep, rocky canyon an hour later, the rancher simply turned off the road, shifted into four-wheel drive, and drove straight down the precipitous slope. We ended up with the truck pretty much nosed into the ground at the bottom of the canyon. That's when the fuel pump conked out. We all piled out of the truck and stood around staring at it, as if that might improve our situation and keep us from freezing to death. My two friends—both of them writers—and the rancher looked deadly serious. I could practically see the terrible thoughts racing through their heads. As for me, I was overcome with an almost unrestrained urge to burst into maniacal laughter! I had to turn and walk away from the group in an effort to conceal my mirth. Had it burst out, my friends would have thought I had gone totally mad out of sheer despair, because they couldn't see anything even slightly amusing in our situation. Not only were they going to freeze to death, they would have to do so in the company of a madman. A bit of ingenuity saved our lives, and I eventually wrote a comic piece about the experience—"The Human Fuel Pump" in *The Grasshopper Trap*.

I don't know why I viewed this rather dreadful situation as being so funny. Maybe it's because some people view the human condition as tragic and others see it as comic. Maybe it's as simple as that, but I don't think so. I certainly don't see the human situation — pain, disease, old age, death, TV talk shows — as comic, or particularly tragic either. Maybe it's that absurdity is the deeper reality of human life, and some of us are born with absurdity detectors, a kind of X-ray vision, a power to see beyond meaning and into lack thereof. I like that. Just thought it up, too. 🚲

Newton: *Got any deep philosophical thoughts about humor, Pat?*

I was afraid you'd never ask, Newt.

Think about this. We *Homo sapiens* are the only earthly creatures possessed of laughter. Perhaps more than anything else, the ability to laugh defines us as human. Scientists once distinguished humans from our predecessors by our ability to make and use tools. We now know that some birds and animals also make and use tools, although I wouldn't recommend any of them for fine cabinetry. There is even some evidence that certain social animals possess behavioral traits akin to ethics, not that a sense of ethics was ever considered a defining characteristic for humans. So it well may be that only laughter distinguishes us as a fundamentally unique life form.

Think what a fine thing it is that only we humans can laugh. Think how annoying it would be if your dog or cat could laugh. You step out of the shower and your cat bursts out laughing. For that very reason, God mercifully deprived animals of a sense of humor.

Think of this. At some point in the ascent of man, the first laugh was heard upon the face of the earth. What was the stimulus that provoked that first laugh? Did someone named Grog slip on a banana peel, to the delight of a fellow caveman, Leroy? Whatever its stimulus, we will never know when and where that first guffaw occurred. Laughter leaves no artifacts. At least I would hope not.

Let us for the moment consider that banana peel Grog may have slipped on. No treatise on humor, by the way, is complete without a discussion of banana peels, which is why I put one in Grog's path. I once read a scholarly paper on humor in which the comedy of slipping on banana peels was discussed and analyzed at considerable length. The author concluded that the perceived humor in the situation results from the frantic efforts of the slippee to defy gravity and thereby preserve his or her dignity, yet another case of reality triumphing over illusion, not to mention the pelvis. Although the paper was one of the more interesting things I've read about the nature of humor, I have never found the spectacle of anyone slipping on anything, no matter the amount of flailing, to be funny in and of itself. To provoke laughter, the comedic situation must be more complex than that.

Take the example of Grog and the banana peel. Our first laugher in the history of the world, Leroy, sees Grog headed toward the banana peel with an armload of sticks for the fire. Leroy thinks, "That stupid Grog is such a show-off—walking erect again!" Suddenly, Grog's feet shoot out from under him and he lands on his back. A weird feeling boils up inside of Leroy and erupts into what we know as a laugh. Leroy previously has witnessed hundreds of falls, without experiencing an urge to laugh, because there is nothing inherently funny about seeing someone fall. What delights Leroy about this fall is his perception of Grog as showing off and the showing off leading to the fall. The "humor" all lies in Leroy's perception of the event, not in anything inherent in the event itself. If Grog had been a sensible caveman like Leroy and gone about on all fours, a mere banana peel wouldn't have caused the slip. The slip being totally unexpected, Leroy, as well as Grog, is caught by surprise and the surprise gives rise to Leroy's involuntary response—laughter. Laughter requires a certain complexity of relationships and perceptions. We'll take up all that in later sessions. Now if you'll excuse me, I'll go lie down. Thinking about the nature of humor always gives me a headache. 🚲

Newton: What do you believe is the ultimate in a prose style, Pat?

It is a style in which the words vanish for the reader. Anytime writing draws attention to itself as writing it detracts from the desired effect, which is to create an uninterrupted flow of thoughts, emotions, images, ideas and information through the mind of the reader.

I have been reading the work of a new young novelist widely acclaimed to be a genius. He certainly seems to be. His writing is dazzling. In fact it is mostly dazzle. I call this "writing writing." It is writing for the sake of writing. Its primary purpose is to call attention to itself. Its secondary purpose is to tell a story. It seems to me that the story should come first. If it is a truly good story, it will stick in the mind forever; it will become part of the reader's life. The words themselves, no matter how dazzling, vanish from memory in an instant. (My theory of style obviously doesn't apply to poetry.)

Many years ago I wrote something like the following in a story, ". . . splashed through shallow pools of sunlight on the trail." I had already formed my theory about prose style, but I loved that image, so much that I could not bear to chop it out, even though I knew that within the context of the story it would be showing off, calling attention to itself at the expense of the real work being done by the other words, phrases and sentences. Several months after the story was published, an English professor I knew mentioned that he had just read that story in a magazine in a dentist's office. "I didn't realize you did fine writing, McManus," he said. "But I came across this wonderful bit of imagery in the story: 'splashing through shallow pools of sunlight on the trail.' Very nice!"

Although savoring the compliment, I knew at that moment that I should have chopped that image. Obviously, it had leaped right up off the page and dazzled the English professor, to the detriment of the story. Shallow pools of sunlight! Just how deep could pools of sunlight be?

For me, a story should flow like a motion picture through the reader's head. Nothing should interrupt the flow of that mind-film, neither fancy footwork by the prose, nor a clumsy sentence, nor a foreign phrase, nor specialized jargon, nor a misplaced comma— nothing. I have never achieved this ideal, often because I like to show off or I'm too lazy to rewrite and rewrite and rewrite until I get a sentence or paragraph just right. But at least I know what I should expect of myself as a writer if I'm to meet the demands of my own theory of style.

Newton: *Is it scary to be a writer, Pat?*

Yes, Newton, it is very scary. Writers live with fear. Some writers cannot deal with the fear, and so they quit or refuse to publish. In order to write, you must either ignore the fear or trick it into leaving you alone. The fear is very sly, though and hard to trick.

The fear in writing comes from exposing your thoughts, your emotions, your experiences, your ideas, your talent, your intelligence, and ultimately your self to public scrutiny and possible scorn. The fear is by no means groundless. You have opened yourself up to the possibility of public humiliations, both by ordinary readers and by paid reviewers who don't like your work because of their tiny, malfunctioning brains.

The need to feed their starving egos is what drives most writers out again and again to expose themselves in pages of print. The need to feed one's self and one's family is a good one, too.

Fear does serve a purpose. It gives the writer the incentive to write his story as well as he or she can. Pride can do that too, but I suspect it comes in a distant second to fear.

I wish I had some magic cure for fear of writing, but I don't. I've known some wonderfully talented writers over the years who could not overcome their fear, and therefore never submitted their work to publishers. Their work was never quite "ready," they'd say. They suffered from fear of failure. And so they kept their great talents hidden from public view. I sometimes wonder if perhaps the greatest novel ever written isn't gathering dust in some filing cabinet somewhere, simply because its author could not overcome the fear of having it published. 🚲

Newton: *Short humor, Pat. What is it and who cares?*

Think of short humor as a brief essay or story with a single purpose: to amuse. It typically appears on the last page of magazines or as syndicated columns in newspapers.

For the past couple of decades, the better-known practitioners of newspaper humor include Erma Bombeck, Dave Barry, Art Buchwald and Mike Royko, all syndicated columnists. Syndication provides such huge audiences that its columnists tend to become far better known than their counterparts in magazines. Newspaper humor columnists are all masters of brevity, as the limited space allowed them demands. Also, they are all consistently funny. Otherwise, they wouldn't be syndicated for very long.

You are not likely to fall down laughing over a newspaper column, with rare exceptions. The limited space doesn't allow for sufficient development of a comic situation to produce that degree of mirth. The newspaper humor column is intended to amuse, to get a chuckle or the occasional guffaw. Tears of merriment seldom course down cheeks in response to a newspaper column.

Probably the best way to land a syndicated column is the way Erma Bombeck did it. She started writing short humor pieces for her local newspaper, no doubt for $5 a column, or less, if I know newspapers. The columns were picked up by other newspapers, her fame and wonderful humor quickly spread, and soon she was syndicated and rich. Very rich.

I was once offered a syndicated column and turned it down. The deal was that I would produce one or two columns a week, my choice. The columns could range in length up to eight-hundred words, my choice. The catch, and there is always a catch, was that I'd be paid according to the number of papers subscribing to the column. It was estimated by the syndicate's sales staff that I would start with about thirty papers, as I recall, and in a year or two work up to a hundred, with the sky the limit after that. I suspected there was also a pie in that sky. As far as I could see, I would work my brain to the bone for at least two years, with very little monetary return for my effort, in other words, about the normal situation for writers. Had I been twenty years younger, I would have jumped at the chance, but I was bearing down on fifty at something approaching the speed of light, or so it seemed—my mid-life crisis flew by so fast my wife didn't even notice—and I decided the amount of work required for a syndicated column would totally dominate the few brief moments remaining to me. If I'd known I'd live this long, I'd probably have accepted the offer.

For a book writer, there is a huge advantage in doing a syndicated column. If you have a syndicated column, you are read by millions of people, all potential book buyers who can instantly be made aware that you have a new book hot off the press. All you have to do is write a column about your harrowing experiences on your recent book promotion tour for your hilarious new book. "A funny thing happened while I was chatting with Larry King. . . ." Right there you've sold one hundred thousand copies. My advice is, if you're offered syndication, take it.

Magazine writers have a better shot at producing tears of merriment, because they have more space than newspaper writers to develop more fully a comic situation. They also get paid much less. More space, less money—you can see how nicely it evens out. Regardless of how funny they might be, newspaper columns live but a day. Because of the nature of newspapers, their humor columns tend to be topical. What's topical today isn't topical tomorrow. Non-topical magazine humor, on the other hand, can last forever, maybe even a year or more.

In writing a humor column for a magazine, I do only one piece a month. Even though I am listed on *Outdoor Life's* masthead as editor-at-large, I am not an employee of the magazine. I remain a freelance writer and contract with the magazine for a certain number of columns per year. As an independent contractor, I am still free to write for other magazines as long as they don't compete directly with *Outdoor Life*.

Writers of magazine short-humor pieces usually will be associated with a particular magazine. James Thurber, Robert Benchley, and S. J. Perelman, for example, wrote mostly for *The New Yorker*, Jean Shepherd mostly for *Playboy*, and Roy Blount, Jr., mostly for *The Atlantic Monthly*, to name but a few of my own favorite short-humor writers.

Short humor is defined mostly by its brevity. Lengths seldom go beyond 2,500 words and usually are much shorter, with many magazines devoting only a single page to a humor column at the back of the publication. The humor can be in the form of stories, essays, commentary or what can only be describe as "pieces."

If you are a funny writer, short humor is probably your best bet for breaking into a magazine. No editor in his right mind will turn down a great piece of humor. The tough part is finding an editor in his right mind. 🚲

Newton: *Pat, do you have any rules for writing humor?*

As a matter of fact I do, Newton. Like most rules, these are made to be broken, but they will generally hold true, even though I just made them up this minute.

1.) Never write about real-life humor. Every so often, I will receive a letter that goes something like this: "We were all going fishing down at the river, and my Uncle Ed, he says he's going to walk a log to get to the other side. Well, about halfway across, Uncle Ed hits a slick patch and his legs shoot out from under him and he goes right in the river. We laughed ourselves sick. You can put this in one of your stories if you want to."

I have no doubt that Uncle Ed's falling in the river was hilarious to those observers on hand. But you will never capture that same hilarity in writing. Real-life humor typically depends upon hundreds, perhaps thousands, of details that you cannot capture in writing: Uncle Ed's personality, what his hair was doing, the sound of his voice, how he was dressed, the expressions on his face, the exact movements of his arms and legs, his body shape, all the relationships between him and the observers of his fall, the depth and temperature of the river, on and on and on. Occasionally an observer, the natural storyteller, can process the event through his own mind and imagination and come up with a version that is actually funnier than the event itself, but in such instances you will usually find that the humor is really a product of the storyteller's art rather than any humor inherent in the event. Also, all the members of the storyteller's audience may be familiar with Uncle Ed and his context in the world. Write up the event, describe it as best you can, and read it to an audience unfamiliar with Uncle Ed, and I suggest you will be very disappointed in the response. The only thing to say then is, "Well, I guess you had to be there." And that is exactly right.

2.) Write about your bad experiences, not your good ones. Write about serious events, not funny ones. Write about your failure, not your success. Write about your fear, not your courage. Write about the negative, not the positive. Write about the bad, not the good. A stingy character is funnier than a generous character. A blow-hard is funnier than a modest character. A mean character is funnier than a kind one. A daffy character is funnier than a sane one. Here is a test: You have been on two camping trips. One turned out to be the most wonderful experience of your life, the other, the worst experience of your life. Which one will you use as the subject for a humor piece?

3.) Write out of your own experience. Most of the humor pieces I write are for *Outdoor Life* magazine. Because I've spent almost my entire life hunting, fishing, camping and roaming about in the Great Outdoors, I have made all the mistakes that it is possible to make. I have committed all the stupidities. When I write about my mistakes and stupidities, my readers recognize them as authentic, because they have done the same dumb stuff. No matter how absurd one of my stories may be, it will contain authentic details the reader will recognize and help him or her to visualize a particular scene. This in turn makes the scene all the more humorous and "real" to the reader. That is why it is important to write out of your own experience.

4.) Use the reader's imagination. The idea here is to provide a few clues about a scene or situation and then let the reader fill in all the rest of the details. Here is a writing exercise I picked up somewhere many years ago. I "create" a complete house with these six words: "tarnished walnut paneling on the stairs." I then ask my students to describe the upstairs of the house, one of its bathrooms, the front yard, and the color of the house. They do so in great detail. Each clearly has a complete house in his or her head. In almost every description, the house will be old but elegant. Often the bathtub in the bathroom will have lion-claw feet. The front yard will often be enclosed by a picket fence in disrepair, and the lawn grass will be dried up and full of weeds. Strangely, a huge tree shows up repeatedly, often with a tire swing hanging from a limb. My point is that those students have imagined a complete house. (They can "see" the house in their heads.) But it is not the same house I hold in my imagination. There are only three features that I want in their varied houses—old, elegant and in disrepair. Here's the point, as I tell my students after the exercise: Use The Reader's House. Even though you may not have any idea what the house looks like, other than the few characteristics you have assigned to it, the reader will have imagined it in complete detail, right down to the flowers on the wallpaper.

Time and again I've had readers tell me, "Your description of such-and-such was so vivid I could actually see it." I have gone back later and reread the "such and such" section, only to discover there was practically no description of the thing mentioned, only a clue or two to trigger a particular image in the reader's mind. You can, of course, manipulate the house in the reader's mind. Perhaps it is important to your story that the house have an attached greenhouse. So give it a greenhouse. But if there is no reason for your character to turn left at the top of the stairs, don't have him turn left. In the house in your reader's mind, it may be impossible to turn left. Suddenly, because of the needless left turn, the reader has to rebuild his house, which fortunately is still pretty fluid in his imagination and not that difficult to rebuild. But if you keep fooling unnecessarily with the reader's imagined house, he will eventually become lost in it, and not know which way to turn, or how to get out of it in case of fire.

Always remember that complete and highly detailed images can arise in the reader's mind from very few carefully selected clues. You furnish the clues, readers will furnish the details. If you want to describe a sleazy motel room, for example, you might want to focus on the cigarette burns in the carpet or on the nightstand, the stains in the sink or on the ceiling, or even more powerful, how the place smells. The reader—at least if he or she has spent as many nights in sleazy motel rooms as I have—will have no trouble arriving at a detailed image of the rest of the room. Writing is always, or should be, a collaboration between the writer and the reader. To make the writing work, the writer must have a keen sense of what the reader can bring to the job. This is particularly true in the writing of humor. Because of its usual brevity, humor requires a major contribution from the reader. For example, I once wrote a story about terrible hunting guides I'd had. One of these guides got both of us lost shortly before nightfall. I wrote something like the following, "As soon as I realized the guide had got us lost, I fired off three quick shots. But the light was bad and I missed him." To set up the readers for the punch line, I needed to misdirect them. My *Outdoor Life* readers know that three shots fired in rapid succession are an emergency signal. Non-hunters may not know that. If I were writing for an audience of non-hunters, I would have had to explain the three shots and give away the joke.

5.) Beware the logic of humor. Even if the story is totally absurd, certain rules of logic apply. In "My First Deer and Welcome to It," the deer escapes by riding my bicycle off down a road and finally disappears over the horizon. In the stage-play version of the story, I later hear that the deer was involved in a shootout—with the police—in Tacoma, Washington—using my rifle! You have to admit that is a pretty absurd situation, but all audiences so far have more than willingly suspended disbelief, to the extent that they become almost crazed with laughter. So where is the logic in this bit of absurdity? It lies in the fact that the deer rides the bike down a road, not off through the woods where fallen trees, rocks and brush would make it impossible to ride a bicycle. How would the deer steer the bike? Its front hooves are tied to each side of the handlebars. How would a deer carry a rifle while riding the bike? The rifle is tied to the handlebars. Even though the scene is absurd, we must take care that the reader's or listener's mental imagery is not destroyed by the writer's failure to take care of certain logical details. No matter how absurd, humor still requires its own particular kind of logic.

6.) Be careful with exaggeration. As you are aware, exaggeration is one of the main tools of humor writing. It seems simple enough at first. For example, my wife, mistaking a coiled rope on the ground for a snake, shoots straight up eight feet in the air. Why eight feet? Because I think that is about right. I could startle her by three times as much and shoot her up twenty-four feet. Twenty-four feet, however, is too exact. It suggests she actually did shoot up that high, that measurements were taken of her peak altitude. It's impossible for anyone to leap straight up twenty-four feet, but it is equally impossible to leap straight up eight feet. In the actual "jump," if there was an actual jump, Bun probably never left the ground. So to say she leaped straight up six inches would be an exaggeration of the actual fact but would still be within the realm of possibility. Exaggeration, generally speaking, should lie outside the realm of possibility but somehow within the realm of visual imagination. Visually can you imagine someone leaping eight feet straight up? Yes you can, even though you know it's impossible. Can you visually imagine someone leaping thirty thousand feet into the air? No, you can't, even though eight feet is no more possible in reality than thirty thousand feet.

Here is how exaggeration works. The reader knows Bun didn't leap straight up eight feet in the air but he still accepts the image of her doing so. In his imagination, he sees her up there in the air, arms and legs flailing, etc. At the same time he knows that the writer shot her up there in the air only for the purpose of suggesting comically her extreme reaction to the sight of the coiled rope on the ground in front of her. The alternative to shooting Bun eight feet up in the air would be to write something like, "She was so scared when she saw that rope on the ground, she gave a little hop and jerked back away from it, and all along it was only a rope, not a snake at all. We laughed and laughed." So here is the deal you make with the reader in the use of exaggeration, you provide him with an impossible comic image for his amusement, but at the same time he interprets that comic image as merely a suggestion to indicate an extreme response to a real-life situation.

In a story called "The Great Cow Plot," I write about how I'm constantly tormented by cows while I'm fishing. It contains this sentence, "If I stop to net a guppy out of a fish tank on the tenth floor of a department store, a cow will get off the elevator and rush over to offer advice." The image of a cow getting off a department-store elevator strikes me as comical. I can "see" it. I hope the reader will pick up a similar image and be amused by it too, while at the same time realizing that this bit of exaggeration is intended to express my irritation over the constant presence of cows in my vicinity anytime I'm fishing.

7.) Don't use a "funny" voice with a tone that keeps saying, in effect, "what I'm telling you is really funny." It's hard to describe, but I'm sure you've heard such a voice. It has a giggle tangled up in it, almost as if the writer is going "hee-hee" every few words. It is also the voice most beginning humor writers employ, in my experience. You will quite often hear bad standup comics use the "funny" voice, particularly if their material isn't funny.

I understand there may be some confusion about what I mean by a writing "voice." Many writers have their own unique voices for writing, voices that are totally different from their normal speaking voices. Hemingway's "voice" is perhaps the most obvious one and for that reason the one most often parodied. Mark Twain had a very distinctive writing voice. Among humor writers, I find each of the following to have his own unique voice: Woody Allen, Robert Benchley, S. J. Perelman and Jean Shepherd, to name a few.

If you are just starting to write humor, you may not have discovered your own unique comic voice yet. No matter. You can invent any number of voices. You can, for example, use a pompous voice, a grouchy voice, an exasperated voice, any voice in fact that suggests a particular kind of character or personality behind it. You might invent a whole new persona for yourself and imagine a voice to go with it. And you can always steal some famous "voice," such as that of Mark Twain, Robert Benchley or any humor writer you particularly like (I wouldn't worry too much that your theft will be recognized). Work at your writing long enough and eventually your own unique voice will emerge.

8.) Use scenes and characters. Most newspaper columnists don't have the luxury of enough space to develop characters and scenes, so they really are confined to writing what amounts to a series of jokes with punch lines. Magazine writers, on the other hand, typically have more space to work with and can therefore develop a more complex kind of humor through the use of characters.

Characters have a tendency to take on lives of their own. Let us say you are working with two characters, each with a distinctive personality of its own. If you place these two characters in a particular situation, each will act consistently with the various characteristics you have provided it. Quite often a surprising chemistry will occur between the two characters, as well as with the situation in which you have placed them, and they will run off with the story, taking it to places you never imagined when you first sat down at the keyboard.

I have been using some of the same characters for about twenty years now. Readers have followed the exploits of Rancid Crabtree for the past couple of decades. He has a history, just like a real person. Readers of my stories can remember predicaments Rancid got himself into fifteen or twenty years ago. Many members of my long-time audience tend to think of him as a real person, as I do myself. When I invented the Rancid character, I based him on an old bachelor who lived near us when I was a kid growing up. I think it is important to base your characters on real people, because that gives them a certain authenticity that may be lacking in a character based solely on imagination. As a matter of fact, many readers have informed me Rancid is a member of their family! And some aren't kidding!

For me, the funniest humor arises out of characters and situations. The greater our familiarity with the character and the situation, the greater the comedy. That is why I find the television program *Frasier* on TV to be profoundly funny. All the actors are superb, of course, but it is the characters and their various relationships that give this comedy such depth. I therefore advise all prospective comedy writers to extract their laughs from characters and situations

9.) Write within a comic idea. But what is a comic idea for a story or essay? In my essay "Sequences," the comic idea is that before you can do anything, you must do something else first, and before you can do that, you must do something else, and so on. In my essay "Temporary Measures," the comic idea is that temporary measures become permanent.

Stories are a bit different. Here the comic idea may have more to do with form than content. For example, you have a story in which the two main characters are constantly bickering and insulting each other. Their actions, however, reveal a great fondness for each other, so irony arises out of the disparity between how they talk to each other and how they act toward each other. Irony is an important ingredient in stories; less so in essays. One way of thinking about irony is in finding the opposite of the expected effect—the kindness that destroys, the cruelty that saves, the greed that gives, the change that remains the same, and so on. Once I have the comic idea for an essay or story, I have no trouble writing it, except for the little drops of blood that bead up on my forehead. Getting the comic idea in the first place, though, can be hard. Very hard.

10.) Never write a list of anything that consists of ten items. Invariably you will run out of steam at item nine.

Newton: *How do book advances and royalties work, Pat?*

Basically, Newton, you license your book to a publishing company, which in exchange pays you a percentage of the cover price of the book—a royalty—for each copy sold. A first-book author typically would get a contract in which the first five thousand copies have a royalty of five percent of the cover price, the second five thousand copies a royalty of ten percent, and the rest of the copies sold a royalty of fifteen percent.

In regard to royalties, old battle-hardened authors like to give young authors these three pieces of advice: 1.) Get the money up front. 2.) Get the money up front. 3.) Get the money up front. In other words, get the biggest advance you can squeeze out of your publisher.

You've probably read of authors getting advances in the many millions of dollars. Chances are that won't happen to you, although I know a young novelist who was paid over a million dollars for a novel. The novel sank like a rock, without leaving so much as a ripple on the reading public's consciousness. Does the author have to return most of the million-plus advance? No, once you get the advance, it's yours, provided you have fulfilled all your contractual obligations.

The phrase "earned back its advance" means that a book has earned enough royalties to equal the advance. A publisher, however, can still make a profit on a book even if the book never earns back its advance.

Publishers are not in the business to lose money, although sometimes it seems as if they are. In regard to royalties, a fifteen percent royalty doesn't mean that you are going to get $3 for every $20 hard-cover of your book sold. No indeed. You usually get that $3 only if the book is sold in a traditional bookstore. Most books nowadays, however, aren't sold in traditional bookstores. They are sold in ware-house stores, department store chains, book clubs, and even on the Internet, often at "excessive discount." In those cases, the royalty typically is cut in half. So in all probability, most of the copies of your book will pay a royalty of one-half the fifteen percent.

You don't care how the publisher sells your book because you already have the advance. The more copies out in the stores, the better it is for you and for the book. After all, you didn't get into this business to make a lot of money anyway, did you? If you do make a lot of money, so much the better, but the main thing is to get your books into the hands of as many readers as possible. 🚴

Newton: Does a first-book author need an agent, Pat?

Somewhere in these pages I tell about how I landed a publisher for my first book without using an agent. Once I had secured a publisher for the book, an agent magically appeared to offer his services. That was back in 1977, when the publishing industry was a kinder, gentler and much simpler place. Today you need an agent. The business is so complex anymore it is almost impossible for anyone but an experienced agent to understand. On my last book contract my agent told me she spent nearly two weeks negotiating the electronic rights alone. I don't even know what electronic rights are. I don't want to know. Anyway, that is why you need an agent.

I suppose it is still possible to interest a publisher in a hot idea for a book, but I doubt the publisher would want to deal directly with you in negotiating a contract. But I don't know. Maybe some would. Once you have a publisher nibbling at your book or book proposal, you will have no trouble landing a good agent.

One way to get an agent is to get acquainted with a well-published author and then ask that author to recommend you to his or her agent. Other authors will hate me for saying that, but it's one of the best ways to get a good agent. I have had students of mine attract the interest of agents by going to writers' conferences in which literary agents are participating as speakers and panelists. The next best thing is to send out book proposals to literary agents and hope that your idea is so good and original that the agent will take you on.

Do be wary of agents who advertise in writing magazines, although for all I know they may be perfectly fine. There are plenty of "literary agencies" that exist for the sole purpose of fleecing writers hopeful of getting their work published. So be careful.

Agents usually take a cut of your advances and royalties—ten to fifteen percent. The agent's commission, by the way, goes on forever. My first agent is still collecting his commission on four of my books—and he's been dead for twelve years! No, I'm not kidding. He was a good agent, though, a really good guy, and my friend, and I hope wherever he is, he is making good use of his commission and not spending it on anything sensible. 🚲

Newton: *Pat, your characters are always yakking away at each other. How come?*

I just enjoy writing dialogue, Newt. It's fun. Sometimes when I have trouble coming up with a story idea, I will put two characters in a scene and start them talking. Often, an idea for the story will emerge from their conversation. It's almost as if I'm eavesdropping on my own characters, my own inventions. How could they know something I don't know? It's weird.

I also eavesdrop on real conversations.

Two cowboys talking over breakfast in a tiny café in Paris, Texas:

"Whatcha been up to, Bo?"

"Been fishin' up Green Lake."

"Fishin'? Green Lake?"

"Yup. Green Lake. Just fishin'."

"So you was fishin' up Green Lake. Huh."

"Yup."

"Them Green Lake fish, there any size to 'em?"

"Oh yeah, good size. For Green Lake."

"What you mean, good size for Green Lake?"

"Well, the fish at Green Lake is usually small, but these was good size."

"For Green Lake?"

"Yeah."

"What's 'good size,' for Green Lake, Bo?"

"Real nice."

At that, I suddenly spun around in my booth, snapped Bo's head back by the hair and held a table fork to his throat. "Now, Bo," I snarled, "tell him how big the damn fish were at Green Lake, and I want pounds, inches and species!"

No, alas, that was only my fantasy, while listening to two cowboys talk while I ate breakfast alone in a little café in Paris, Texas. Somewhere, somehow, I knew I would use their "conversation." I have not here tried to duplicate it but only to capture certain nuances that reveal its basic inanity.

In writing dialogue, I try to suggest the way certain people talk, to capture certain characteristics that seem to distinguish their speech. You can easily overdo this. Years ago I made a terrible mistake in trying to duplicate as exactly as I could the speech of the individual one of my characters, Rancid Crabtree, is based upon. The real Rancid, as it happened, had grown up far back in the Appalachian Mountains and was pretty much your classic hillbilly. For a while, I kept my own little Rancid lexicon to keep track of how he pronounced certain works, such as "hyar" for "here" and "fahr" for "fire." But if Rancid said "maw" for "my" shouldn't he also say "skaw" for "sky" and "baw" for "buy?" It became a nightmare, and I eventually gave up on consistency. Rancid still says "maw" for my" but not "skaw" for "sky." I now try to suggest only a few of his distinguishing speech sounds and patterns, which is easier on both me and the reader. (A California graduate student taking a course in linguistics once analyzed Rancid's speech for a paper he was writing. He concluded that most uneducated people in Idaho talk like Rancid Crabtree.)

If you have ever listened to a tape recording of a meeting, you realize what a mess human discourse is. Transcriptions of these recordings must surely be the most boring reading anyone has yet devised. Participants start sentences they never finish. Points under discussion are left behind in endless digressions and digressions from digressions, and the points are never heard from again. Definitely do not try to duplicate actual human speech in your writing.

I once listened to a tape of some people who were apparently smoking pot. At one point a voice pipes up, "What say we go get . . ." This is followed by some other voices arguing about politics or something. At least ten minutes pass. Then the piping voice says, ". . . a hamburger?" If I ever have need to create a dialogue among some pot smokers, I will remember to drop that in somewhere.

What you should listen for are unusual expressions, different rhythms of speech, strange pronunciations, unusual patterns, repetition of certain phrases, etc., so that you can make each "voice" in your dialogues distinctive and different from all the others.

Dialogue can contribute so much not only to personalities in a story but also to places. Here are waitresses from two different eating establishments talking. What can you tell about each place from the way each waitress speaks?

"May I take your order now sir, or would you like a few more minutes?"

"What's it gonna be, Honey?"

Which of the two places offers to grind fresh pepper over your salad? Which has tablecloths? Which identifies men's and women's restrooms as "Guys" and "Dolls?"

Dialogue is extremely useful to the writers of all fictive works, whether novels, short stories or short-humor pieces, because it does so many things all at the same time.

1.) Dialogue itself may be funny or otherwise entertaining and thereby hold the interest of the reader.

2.) It helps develop the personalities of characters as they speak.

3.) It provides information to advance the story.

4.) It can be a vehicle for irony and obscurity.

"As the Ear is Bent" is a little piece I wrote using only one side of a two-person dialogue. The other side is implied. Nevertheless, I think the reader can guess the responses of the neophyte outdoorsman, Newton, even though we never hear him actually speak.

Note the obscurity in the piece. The "real" situation of the story is "obscured" by the Old Geezer (OG). All the reader can know about the situation is what the OG reveals. But the OG is not reporting just the facts. He is giving his own little spin to the various occurrences. I, the writer, expect the reader to "see through" the OG and perhaps even see through Newton seeing through him. Because of the obscuring by the OG, the reader has to interpret for himself, among other things, why Newton ends up with less hair every time he lights the OG's old gas lantern and finally kicks the lantern over the tent.

As is often the case in this kind of short humor, the comic idea and the comic form are one and the same. The humor of the piece depends upon the Old Geezer's obscuring our direct perception of the situation.

The obscurity here may also be thought of as weak irony, as opposed to the kind of in-your-face irony one comes across in the literary short story or novel. Weak irony (I just invented the term) means simply that the comments of the OG reveal the opposite of what he intends them to. His own words undermine his pretenses.

By the way, I didn't try to put together a set of qualities and characteristics for the OG that would gradually add up to a particular personality as he talks. The character was in my mind, and I simply let him reveal himself as he was—or is.

Oddly enough, in reading over this story several months after it was written, I was surprised how much of the personality of *Newton's* character comes through, even though we never hear him speak or see him. While I was writing it, I didn't give much thought to Newton's personality at all, because I never intended him to be heard from. But words work their own chemistry, and you can never be quite sure what they are cooking up for you.

Newton: Can you define "humor," Pat?

No. I could give it a shot, though.

I suppose you could say that humor is anything that amuses people, makes them smile or laugh. Some people do laugh at some very ugly and cruel things, though. Can a public hanging serve as comedy? Apparently it does, or once did. Nobody ever said humor had to be nice. Perhaps part of the delight in audiences at a public hanging came from feelings of relief over not being the guest of honor, or maybe feelings of superiority, "I may have had a bad day but his is worse." Hanging—the ultimate put-down.

Humor arise out of language, if we extend the concept of language to include images. No language, no humor.

Humor does not occur in nature. Dogs and cats, pigs and cows never laugh. It's a good thing, too. Imagine trying to milk a cow that could laugh. How would you feel about eating a pot roast that had once guffawed at your jokes?

Humor is far more complex than tragedy and taps into more complex emotions It requires more mental and emotional dexterity, more intelligence.

A while back I was working on a comedy script with another writer. He said, "I think we need more poignance." What we needed were more laughs. Poignance is ten cents a ton. "If we need poignance," I said, "we'll kill the family dog."

I hate poignance.

When did humor get its start? Imagine the eerie sound of that first laugh ringing out upon the earth. I bet that turned some heads.

Lots of creatures can cry. Only man can laugh. He seems defined by his laughter. Possibly even more by hers.

Laughter is not only the best medicine but the best revenge, although being rich and handsome and outliving all your enemies are good ones, too.

Newton: Is pain funny?

I hate to admit it, Newton, but pain can be funny, at least in stories. Each of us, or most of us anyway, may have a touch of the Marquis de Sade in us. Actually, it isn't so much that the pain itself is funny, but the response to pain.

A man lying in bed and moaning in agony from a headache isn't funny, of course. No? Wait a minute. Suppose the headache is the result of drinking too much the night before, the less messy part of a severe hangover. Right, you've seen that scene a hundred times on TV and in films, put there for comic effect. You probably laughed at it, too. Don't try to kid me. And suppose the headache is about to get a whole lot worse: The man's disgruntled wife appears at the head of the bed holding a huge bell and a hammer and announces, "At the sound of the gong, breakfast will be served."

In reality, the sight of a person, even your worst enemy, writhing in agony is not conducive to mirth. A story, however, is not reality. Or perhaps it creates its own reality, with a different set of rules than those generally found in normal reality.

As you have probably noticed, pain is a major comic ingredient in animated cartoons featuring Wyle E. Coyote and the Roadrunner. I'm sure you've heard audiences roaring with laughter at the sight of Wyle getting blown up, burnt to a crisp, flattened, squished and so on. Why is that funny? Extreme pain—and death!—Would have to accompany any of those conditions in real life. Why does cartoon pain amuse? Here are my guesses:

First, the characters are cartoons and can't feel real pain.

Second, Wyle has brought each disaster on himself. He isn't the victim but the villain, whose treacherous devices backfire on him. He deserves what he gets.

Third, Wyle's response is not appropriate to the damage done to him. He doesn't, for example, scream in agony after being flattened to the thickness of a pancake but instead races about in his flattened state, making little squeaking sounds.

It is important to keep these points in mind while writing about pain in a comic story. If either the pain or the character are too realistic, the comic aspects will be lost.

Here is how I dealt with pain in one of my stories, "Poof! No Eyebrows!"— from *Never Sniff a Gift Fish*. It is a story about my fooling around with black powder as a teenager. My crowning achievement is the construction of a sewer-pipe cannon, with which my friend Retch Sweeney and I set out to fire a croquet ball down a golf course fairway. The cannon blows up the instant we light the fuse. A deputy sheriff shows up seeking the cause of the explosion. He finds Retch and me recovering behind a utility shed.

"Now, what I want to know," the deputy went on, "is why you two boys are sitting out behind this shed smoking."

"Shucks," I said. "If you'd been here a little earlier you'd have seen us while we were still on fire."

There is, of course, the misdirection through the use of the word "smoking" for the purpose of creating a little surprise. If the boys have been on fire, they are obviously in pain, but the obvious pain in the situation has been pushed to the background in the dialogue between the boys and the deputy. Compare that approach to, say, a vivid and direct description of the boys screaming and thrashing about on the ground while they try to smother their burning clothes. Not funny. If you think so, seek help.

Remember that pain can be hilarious if properly handled in the comic story, but it can be very tricky, indeed. It is easy for an author to come off looking like a monster, when he attempts to treat pain comically. I suggest that when you use pain for comic effect, it should be very much like cartoon pain.

Newton: *Pat, what about timing, anticipation and surprise in the writing of comedy?*

As I'm sure you've heard, Newton, timing is everything. Well, maybe not *everything*. Nothing is everything.

Timing is much easier to control in live performances than it is in writing. In performance, for example, a pause in delivery can be hilarious. Jack Benny had a great pause in one of his shows. I've heard that pause produced the longest stretch of continuous laughter in the history of radio. The Jack Benny character had the reputation of being an enormous skinflint. In this skit, a robber accosts Jack in an alley. "Your money or your life!" he snarls. This is followed by a long pause from Jack, as he tries to make a decision between his life and his money. The audience goes berserk over his silence. How do you write a pause like that into a page of print? Obviously, you can't simply leave a bunch of white space for the reader to contemplate.

One way is to arouse anticipation in the reader that something is about to happen. It happens, but you don't tell the reader right away *what* happened. You continue with other aspects of your story. The reader's anticipation of the punch line is put on hold. Let's suppose one of your characters, Ed, stops by a house to ask directions. Another character, Bill, says, "Better watch out Ed, that dog looks real mean."

"Don't worry about that," Ed replies, walking through the gate. "You just have to let a dog know who's boss. Down, boy, dow—!"

You, the writer, don't tell the reader immediately what happened but instead leap ahead to a later point in time. The reader is thus left in a state of suspended expectation. In other words, there is a pause between the time the event happens and the time the reader finds out what occurred.

Is that clear? I hope so, because I don't want to run through it again.

Reader anticipation and surprise are important elements in humor, and both depend upon just the right timing. The idea is to lead readers to anticipate one thing and then surprise them with another.

In the Roadrunner animated cartoons, for example, Wyle E. Coyote sets his traps for the speedy Roadrunner, usually in a three-part sequence: 1.) He paints a picture of a tunnel on a solid rock wall, hoping Roadrunner will try to run through the fake tunnel and then smack into the wall. 2.) Roadrunner zooms right through the tunnel. 3.) Amazed, Wyle takes a run at the same tunnel and flattens himself against the picture on the rock. The audience anticipates a three-element sequence, because that is the form gags take in almost all animated cartoons.

In the next segment, however, Wyle appears with a bomb to drop on the Roadrunner. The audience is anticipating another three-part sequence: 1.) Wyle lights the fuse—BOOM! The animators have surprised the audience with a one-element gag. They have anticipated the audience's anticipation of a certain sequence and surprised it by eliminating the sequence. Surprise often can trigger a spontaneous laugh at even the weakest of jokes, and here it achieves the surprise with a change in the timing.

The writer of humor must think constantly about ways to surprise the reader, to catch him off guard. Here is another example. One of my characters is a smelly old woodsman, Rancid Crabtree. In describing Crabtree, I once used a sentence that went something like this, "He chewed and spat tobacco, drank homemade whiskey, told outrageous lies, never worked, never took baths, never got up before noon and in general seemed to be the ideal role model for me."

The first part of the sentence leads the reader to anticipate disapproval from young Pat but instead is surprised by his *approval* of Rancid's lifestyle. The main function of the sentence, however, is not to surprise the reader but to describe the old woodsman. The surprise adds a bit of entertainment to the sentence's primary purpose, in this case, description. The "joke," for lack of a better word, dominates the sentence, but at the same time the reader has absorbed important details about the character.

Surprise and anticipation are basic to comedy. Babies a few weeks old can get a great laugh out of a game of peekaboo. A baby, surprised by the first few peekaboos soon learns to anticipate the next peekaboo. The anticipation can delight it as much as the surprise when it comes. If the timing of the peekaboos is unvaried, however, the baby will soon become bored, because it is no longer surprised. Timing is everything, even with peekaboo. Oh, I forgot. Nothing is everything.

Newton: So, Pat, what's the highest high in writing? The lowest low?

Speaking for myself, the highest high is to write a comedy for a live performance on stage and then hear the audience respond with roars of laughter. The lowest low is to write a comedy for a live performance on stage and NOT hear the audience respond at all!

Six or seven years ago, I ran into actor Tim Behrens, who suggested that I adapt some of my stories for the stage. I thought that sounded like a pretty good idea. I did nothing about it though. Time passed. Then one day Behrens called me up and said, "Guess what? I've reserved the Panida Theater for a performance of our play next October." So then I had to write the script, "A Fine and Pleasant Misery: The Humor of Patrick McManus." The script wasn't so much a play as a one-man show, similar to what Hal Holbrook has done in "Mark Twain Tonight."

Opening night, the theater was packed. I was terrified. Tim was terrified. What madness had got into us that we would actually think something like this might work? But it did work. The audience responded with great rolling waves of laughter. It was wonderful.

Tim has now performed the play in cities in about twenty states, as far east as Detroit and as far south as Dallas. The "play" is still going strong in its seventh year of performances and has now been joined by another play, "McManus in Love," which more accurately can be described as a "play." Paid attendance has reached approximately 150,000 for both plays. Not bad for two guys from Spokane, Behrens and McManus, who for some reason actually thought they could create a piece of theater.

Touring a play is no bed of roses. It is fraught with risk, financial, physical, emotional—and the biggest risk of all, that you won't get a laugh. But it is exciting.

One of the great advantages that writing for the stage has over writing for print is that you get to see what works and what doesn't work. If a line doesn't get a laugh, you can either tinker with it or write a whole new line and try it out at the next performance. Once a line is in print, though, it might as well be set in concrete. But that doesn't matter anyway, because you never get to hear your print audience respond to it. You almost never know if a line in print works, but there is no doubt about the line delivered on stage before an audience. Behrens and I now feel that a play must go through at least thirty performances before it takes on its final form. Even then, Behrens will sometimes forget a line and have to fill in with an ad-lib. Sometimes the ad-lib gets a better response than the original line, and so it is added to the script. (This doesn't happen nearly as often as Behrens claims!)

Creating a play is always a collaboration involving the writer, the actor and the director. Tim and I have been most fortunate in having Jack Delehanty as the director of our plays. The director seldom gets much credit but it is he who gives shape, form and fine tuning to the work of the writer and actor. He also serves as the arbitrator in disputes between writer and actor, of which there are seldom more than a few thousand per play.

I see no reason why any writer-actor-director team could not create and stage a one-man show of some kind. You need only do what Tim, Jack and I did. You write a script, the actor learns the script, the director shapes the performance. Then you go rent a theater, advertise your show in the local newspaper and on radio, and the next thing you know, the curtain is going up. You are about to experience the highest of highs. Or the lowest of lows.

I have learned more about writing from doing the plays than anything I've ever done before. One of the most important things I've learned is that the devil is in the details. For example, we had a line in one of the plays that should have worked but never did. The audience simply would not respond to it. Then Tim's wife, Leslie Grove, suggested that we change the verb in the sentence from present tense to past tense.

We did. Presto! The line now got the expected laugh. Go figure.

Working on the plays further confirmed for me that the medium in which the fictive writer works is the imagination of the audience. With both my books and the plays, I depend upon the imagination of the audience to furnish most of the visual detail in the action and scenes. The audience is given a few clues and must then contribute the rest from the imagination. It is quite amazing how vividly the audience's imagination creates a particular thing or scene when in fact all they are looking at is an actor on an essentially bare stage. One night after a performance that involved a bicycle, a little boy rushed up to Tim, and hardly containing his amazement, said, "Mr. Behrens! Mr. Behrens! I have a bicycle *exactly* like that one in your show!" Not only was there no actual bike on the stage, the one in the performance had not even been described. For that little boy, the bicycle in the performance was indeed exactly like the one he had at home, because it was one and the same bike.

I have never had a better lesson in how words work upon the imagination. 🚲

Newton: *I hear people putting down slapstick comedy, Pat. Why is that? For that matter, what is slapstick?*

My *Random House Dictionary of the English Language* has a pretty good definition of "slapstick," Newt, so I'll use it:

> 1. broad comedy characterized by violently boisterous actions, as the throwing of pies in actor's faces, mugging, and obvious farcical situations and jokes; farce combined with horseplay in a comic form. 2. a stick or lath used by harlequins, clowns, etc., as in pantomime, for striking other performers, esp. a combination of lath that makes a loud clapping noise without hurting the person struck.

It's true, Newt, that you often hear someone putting down slapstick because of its lack of sophistication. "Oh, that's just slapstick comedy," as though slapstick is far beneath them and suited only for the vulgar masses. Then the person might add with a superior sniff, "Actually, I myself prefer British comedy." Ha! The fact is that British comedy is made up almost entirely of slapstick! The work of Benny Hill and Monty Python comes to mind as examples, but British comedy is thoroughly saturated with slapstick, some of it exquisitely gross, with frequent departures into basic bathroom humor. Brits (and children!) love their bathroom humor almost as much as they do their slapstick. Oddly enough, Americans, generally thought to be much more vulgar than the English, seem generally not amused by bathroom humor and even put off by it. But enough about that. I simply want to make the point here that one of the reasons American comedies, either on film or TV, are seldom funny is that their producers make a deliberate effort to avoid slapstick, no doubt because they believe it too gauche for their own refined sense of the artistic. On the rare occasion when they do use some slapstick, they almost always get laughs. Just any old slapstick won't do, of course. The director and actors must have a genius for slapstick, just as for any other form of comedy.

Stories with Commentaries

Newton: *How do you know if something you have written is funny, Pat?*

You don't Newt. It is a mystery we can never fathom but only sense, as in *sense* of humor. As I mention elsewhere in this book, the writing of humor is rather scary because you have no way of knowing that what you have written is actually funny. Just because you, the writer, think it's funny doesn't mean anyone else in the entire world will think so. The risk is real. If the humor piece you've written turns out not to be funny, your ego can end up flatter than roadkill, your psyche a mere grease spot on the wall of literature. Of all the different forms of writing, nothing is more dreadful than the humor piece that tries to be funny but fails. I like to say that humor is the most existential of all writing, not merely because that sounds good but because the response to it is, well, so *existential*—laughter. The flowing prose, the deft turn of phrase, the clever figure of speech, the subtle symbolism, all mean nothing without the laugh, or its lesser sibling, the smile. Ultimately, your only guide for what is funny is your own instinct, your own *sense* of humor.

"A Good Deed Goes Wrong"

Some people thought Crazy Eddie Muldoon and I were to blame for breaking Rancid Crabtree's leg. Oddly, the odorous and crotchety old woodsman himself was one of the people who thought this. He said as soon as he got off his crutches he intended to run Eddie and me down and whale the tar out of us. We weren't too worried. We figured by the time Rancid got out of the cast he would have cooled off enough to see that the accident was really his own doing and no fault of ours. But before he got off his crutches, the little incident with the bobcat occurred, generally confusing matters even more. As Crazy Eddie observed at the time, you try to do a kind deed for a person, and it just gets you into more trouble. Anyway, here are the true facts about the entire mess.

During our Christmas vacation from the third grade, Eddie and I built a toboggan run up on the mountain behind Rancid's shack. The design of our run was based on the one we had seen in newsreels at the Pandora Theater the Saturday before. The two runs were almost identical, except ours was steeper and faster than the one in the newsreel, and went over and under logs and had brush on both sides of it, and at least one of the turns was much sharper, and if you didn't make that turn you would be shot off into space and sail for some time over the valley looking down at the tiny cows and cars beneath you, and this in turn might elevate your anxiety to a dangerous level. So you wanted to be sure to make that sharp curve.

We built the first part of the run on an old logging road that zigzagged down the mountain. We tramped up and down the road the distance of two switchbacks, packing down the snow into a track slightly wider than the width of our sled. The grade on the switchback was modest, but sufficient to build up a fair head of speed in a sled by the time it and its driver reached the curve at the end of the second switchback. Then came the good part. Instead of curving the track onto the next switchback, we funneled it over the edge of the road into an old skid trail.

The skid trail had been gouged into the mountain by old-time loggers dragging logs down it. In fact, it was so steep they probably didn't have to drag the logs but merely had to roll them into it and let them shoot to the bottom of the mountain. Erosion had cut the trail down to bare rock, which was now coated with ice, making it even better for the toboggan run. When we were building up our curved bank to funnel the track into the skid trail, Eddie slipped and nearly shot down the run with nothing but his body, and would have if he hadn't managed to grab a small tree and pull himself back up.

"Wow!" he said. "This is going to be good!"

At the bottom end, the skid trail intersected with the next switchback of the road. This was where the toboggan driver would shoot off into space if he failed to make the turn onto the switchback. Fortunately, there was a high bank on the downhill side of the road, only slightly offset from the track. The driver would have to be alert enough to steer toward the high bank, which would sweep the sled up and around and then redirect it back down onto the switchback. This was the last switchback and it provided a straightaway that, at the bottom, merged with the Sand Creek Road. The straightaway was quite steep, so the toboggan driver wouldn't have to worry about his speed diminishing any when he hit this last stretch. He could then glide to a gradual stop on the Sand Creek Road, which was seldom traveled during winter, and even then only by old Mrs. Swisher, who drove to church on it each Sunday. We completed the track on a Friday, and planned to make our first test run Saturday.

The next morning, Crazy Eddie and I were dragging my sled past Rancid's shack on our way up to test our toboggan run and were arguing about who got to go down first.

"Listen, Eddie, it's my sled!" I said.

"Yeah, that's right," he replied. "That's why you should get to be first to test the run."

"No sirree," I said. "I should be the one who gets to choose who goes first, and I choose you."

About then Rancid stuck his head out the door of his shack. "What you boys up to now?" he hollered at us. "Some kinder monkey bidness, no doubt. Ah ain't never seen no younguns who could get into more trouble than you two."

"We built a toboggan run up on the mountain, just like in the newsreel, Rancid. It's fast too."

"Hold up a sec," he said, putting on his coat. "Ah better go check this out. You fool half-pints probably invented some new way to kill yersevs."

Half an hour later, we stood at the start of the toboggan run, all of us still puffing great clouds of vapor from the climb up the trail.

Rancid stared at the little track going down the first switchback. It didn't look nearly so impressive this morning. "Shoot," he said, chuckling. "You call this a toboggan run? Ah caint believe Ah clumb all the way up hyar to see this piddlin' little trail in the snow. Ah must hev been outta maw mind. Gimme thet sled. The least you can do is let me ride to the bottom of the mountain on it."

I handed over the sled. Rancid plopped down on it, sitting upright with his long legs sticking way out in front, his coat completely concealing the sled beneath him.

"It might be dangerous, Mr. Crabtree," Eddie warned.

"Dangerous!" Rancid said. "Eddie, Ah 'spect Ah never told you, but Ah used to be a professional bobsledder, jis like you see in the movies. Racin' Rancid they used to call me."

"Gee." I said. "I didn't know that." I figured that he must have been a professional bobsledder right after being a fighter pilot and before he became a big-game hunter in Africa or about the same time he was a champion prize fighter.

"Yep," Rancid said, poking a wad of chewing tobacco into his cheek. "Now gimme a shove off."

He glided slowly away toward the first curve, gradually picking up speed. He called back to us as he went around the curve. "Ah hate to tell you this, boys, but your bobsled track ain't steep enough even to give a feller a decent ride."

We were disappointed in the professional bobsledder's assessment of our run but thought his opinion of it might improve later on. Sure enough, the next time we heard him yell was about when we thought he should hit the funnel into the skid trail.

"Gol-DAAAAAAA-a-a-n-n-n-g-g-g-g!"

"I think he liked the skid-trail section," Eddie said.

"Yeah," I said. "He sounded excited."

So that is how Rancid broke his leg. He said later he didn't know when, where, or how he broke his leg, or even that he had, because his mind was so occupied with other matters, among which was whaling the tar out of Eddie and me at the first opportunity.

The only eyewitness other than Rancid was old Mrs. Swisher, who was a little daft anyway and really couldn't be relied on for an accurate observation. "I got a little mixed up," she related, "and thinking it was Sunday instead of Saturday, I started driving to town to go to church. As always, I was especially nervous going by that dreadful Rancid Crabtree's shack, because he's in cahoots with the devil. Well, I'm driving along real careful minding my own business when all the sudden that fool Crabtree zooms right by me, just flying he was, about a foot in the air, going like the wind. I just caught a glimpse of his face, he was going so fast, and I'm sorry I did, because it had such a hideous expression on it you can't even imagine! The thought of it has kept me awake nights ever since. And he's holding this little green tree in one hand, torn right out by the roots it was. I bet the tree has something to do with one of those devilish rites of his. Well, he shot off down Sand Creek Hill and I thought he might be laying in ambush for me up ahead, so I turned right around and went home, and it was a good thing I did, too, because then I remembered it was Saturday instead of Sunday."

Naturally, nobody took daft Mrs. Swisher's account seriously, although Eddie and I did recover my sled at the bottom of Sand Creek Hill, where it had shot off over the bank and landed on the frozen creek. Sprayed out in front of it was what we first thought to be blood but then discovered was nothing more interesting than tobacco juice.

A couple of Saturdays later, Eddie and I were walking along the highway pulling my sled, the runners of which were somewhat splayed, but still worked. We had been trying to come up with an idea for making amends with Rancid, when we saw a furry shape lying in the highway. Both of us had fine road kill collections and this specimen looked exceptional.

"It's mine," I said as we rushed forward. "You got the last one."

"No sirree," Eddie said. "I remember. You got the nice flattened toad last fall and . . . Hey, what is this anyway?"

"My gosh, it's a bobcat. Feel it. It must have just been killed. It's still warm. Look, it's got a bit of blood on its head where the car hit it, but otherwise it's in great shape. Well, I'd better take my bobcat home. Maybe I'll stuff it."

"No, you won't," Eddie said. "I'm gonna take it home and stuff it."

"Hey, wait a minute," I said. "I know what. We'll give it to Rancid. He can skin it and sell the hide. Then he won't be mad at us anymore. What do you say Eddie?"

Eddie reluctantly agreed. We loaded the bobcat on my sled and hauled it over to Rancid's shack. I pushed the door gently open and peeked inside, to make sure Rancid wasn't close enough to swat me before he saw we had brought him a gift. The old woodsman was still in bed, snoring loudly, his casted foot sticking out from under the covers and resting on a block of firewood. He had pulled a red wool stocking cap over his bare foot where it stuck out of the cast.

"Rancid's still asleep," I whispered to Eddie. "Should we wake him up?"

Crazy Eddie grinned. "Naw, he's probably all pooped out from dragging that cast around with him. Let's just carry the bobcat in and put it on the table next to his bed, so he can see it when he first wakes up. It'll be a nice surprise for him."

Eddie was very good at thinking up nice surprises for people. We carried the bobcat in and laid it down on the table next to the snoring Rancid. Eddie studied the arrangements.

"No good," he whispered. "It looks too dead." He looked around and found a box of kitchen matches. Then he took out two of the matches and used them to prop apart the big cat's lips in a pretty fair imitation of a snarl. Then he stuck the matchbox under the animal's chin so it looked as if the bobcat were holding its head up, ready to spring. Then we tiptoed out and hunkered alongside the door to await the old woodsman's awaking.

"I think he's gonna be real surprised," Eddie said.

"Yeah, me too."

Presently, Rancid stopped snoring. He muttered something in his sleep. Then he apparently banged the table with his arm, because we heard a bump and then the sound of the matchbox hitting the floor.

"Darn," Eddie whispered. "The matchbox fell out from under the bobcat's chin. The surprise is ruined now."

"Whazzat?" Rancid mumbled. "What in tarnation . . . GOL-DANG! GIT! GIT AWAY FROM MEEE!"

Eddie and I chuckled.

The table crashed to the floor. A chair was flung against the wall and a block of firewood sailed out the door. All of this was accompanied by a terrible roaring and snarling and the wildest cussing I had ever heard.

"GIT BACK! GIT BACK!" Rancid yelled amid the bangs and crashes and thumps.

Eddie looked at me. "I didn't think he'd be this surprised."

"No fooling," I said nervously. "Maybe we'd better leave right now. We can tell him later about our present for him, when he isn't so surprised."

At that moment, there was a furious rattling of the crutches and Rancid burst out of the shack, shot across the yard and into his privy, slamming the door shut behind him.

Eddie and I were so started we couldn't move. Then the bobcat walked out the door, chewing on a match stick. It gave us a contemptuous glance and went off up the mountain shaking its head, either because it had a headache or because it couldn't believe what it had just witnessed.

Rancid opened the privy door a crack and watched the bobcat until it disappeared in the woods. Then he saw us. Crazy Eddie and I started toward home.

"You ever seen Rancid move that fast before?" Eddie asked.

"Nope," I said, glancing back over my shoulder. "Specially not on crutches."

"Didn't even use his legs," Eddie said, with a touch of awe. "Had those ol' crutches whippin' around like spokes on a wheel. Do you think he was ever an acrobat in a circus?"

"Probably."

"I see he don't sleep in pajamas neither," Eddie said, puffing clouds of vapor into the icy air.

"Yeah," I said, panting my own clouds of vapor. "He probably will after this though."

We passed daft old Mrs. Swisher's car askew on the road below Rancid's shack. She was staring vacantly at us, her mouth hanging open.

"It's Saturday, Mrs. Swisher," Eddie yelled as we sped past. "Sunday ain't till tomorrow."

She didn't reply. But I could tell she was going to have trouble getting to sleep again that night. It isn't often you see a naked man on crutches with a red stocking cap on his foot chase two boys through the snow on a cold winter morning. What was even stranger, the crippled old woodsman kept gaining on us.

Commentary

"A Good Deed Goes Wrong" has turned out to be one of my most popular stories, both in print and on the stage. I'm not sure what elements in the story produced this exceptional response from audiences, but I suspect it has something to do with the relationship between the devious Eddie and the good-hearted but boastful Rancid. The reader is allowed to see through the pretensions of both characters. Eddie knows full well that the skid trail section of the toboggan run is dangerous. When he warns Rancid— "It might be dangerous, Mr. Crabtree"— he knows full well that Rancid won't take the warning seriously. Eddie is a trickster operating undercover as a little boy. When Eddie places the bobcat right next to the sleeping Rancid's head, he lets on that he is performing a good deed and that his expectation is that Rancid will be delighted with the gift when he sees it.

I make use of an "observer" in this story. An "observer," in the sense that I use the term, is someone who sees only a small section of a whole series of events that may appear logical enough if you've seen the whole series up to that point but may be totally outrageous and mystifying if you only see a tiny portion. In this story, of course, the observer is Mrs. Swisher, who gives her own report of the event to the sheriff. "Observers" are very useful in the writing of humor.

One of the great things about having your work performed on stage is that you get to see an audience respond to it. I have watched my actor, Tim Behrens, perform this story dozens of times, and he absolutely knocks the audience out with it. Throughout, the audience has a building sense of anticipation but without being quite sure what is about to happen. This story and several others that are also performed on stage have led me to believe that creating anticipation, or suspense, in the audience can lead to the most intense kind of laughter. One of the things that has amazed me the most about this story as it is performed on stage is the audience's response to "the little green tree." I planted this little green tree at the top of the skid trail just for the purpose of having it show up again later in the story. It was important that the image of Eddie pulling himself back up the skid trail with "the little green tree" stick in the reader's or viewer's mind. When Mrs. Swisher mentions that Rancid is holding "a little green tree" when he zooms past her, the audience almost falls out of its seats. The response is instantaneous. In the second or two it takes Mrs. Swisher to say the phrase, the image of Rancid tearing out that tree in a desperate attempt to save himself leaps full-blown into the viewer's imagination. Clearly, the tiniest detail or suggestion can have a powerful effect on an audience. In the writing of humor, I am convinced that less is almost always more. Now if I can just remember that.

Newton: *Pat, what do you think your most famous story is, or is that something impossible to judge?*

If you had asked me to select my funniest story, I couldn't even have guessed at an answer, because there is such variation in what people think is funny. As to the most "famous" of my stories, meaning the story familiar to the most people, I have no problem with that. It is "The Deer on a Bicycle."

The story was originally published in *Field & Stream* magazine under the title "My First Deer and Welcome to It." Later the story was included in a collection of my humor pieces, *They Shoot Canoes, Don't They?*, published by Henry Holt and Company, Inc. After that, it was published in *Reader's Digest* and selected for several anthologies. It has been recorded on both video and audio tapes and translated into several foreign languages. Finally, I adapted it for the stage, which is the version used here.

I have written three one-man shows in which I've adapted many of my short-humor pieces for the stage, where they are performed by actor Tim Behrens. Some pieces that are funny in print, I've discovered, aren't particularly funny on stage. On the other hand, some pieces that are only mildly funny in print become hilarious on stage. "The Deer on a Bicycle" works great for both.

"Deer" presents all sorts of problems for the actor. For the story to work using nothing but a bare stage, he has to create in the mind of the audience a deer, a bike, a hunting camp and even a mountain. All of these elements must come together vividly in the audience's imagination. The degree to which he succeeds is evident from the reaction of the little boy, who, as I mentioned earlier, after a performance cried out in amazement, "I have a bicycle exactly like that one!" And of course he did. That was his very own bike, the bicycle his imagination had contributed to the performance.

"The Deer on a Bicycle"

One of the props on stage is a box containing memorabilia from Pat's childhood. On orders from Pat's wife, Bun, he is supposed to be sorting through the contents and discarding items that no longer have any use or meaning to him. He discards nothing. At this point, he reaches into the box and pulls out an old metal deer tag.

Oh, hey! What's this? Wow! You don't see these things anymore. An old metal deer tag. Now the tags are all made out of cardboard you have to punch and fill out. Takes less paperwork to check into a hospital. Hunting's not so much fun anymore either. When I was young and my family was poor, boy, if I brought home a deer, it was cause for a major celebration. I was treated like a . . . a . . . hero! But if I bring home a deer now, all my daughters start screaming and crying, "Dad snuffed Bambi!"

"No no," I explain. "He was hit by a truck on the highway and I was rushing him to the vet when he suddenly expired on the front seat of my car. So we'll hold a short memorial service. And then we'll eat him.

"Nooo! You cannibal!"

But it was different in the olden days. When I was fourteen, I loved deer hunting more than anything I could think of. I only had two problems: I had never been and I didn't have anyone to take me. Remember, my dad had died when I was very young, and none of the neighbors, not even Rancid Crabtree, wanted to be around me when I was armed. There were no deer near where I lived, so I decided the only thing to do was to ride my bicycle up into the mountains and go hunting by myself.

Pantomime tying rifle to handlebars and then pumping bike up mountain.

The next morning I tied my rifle to the handle bars of my bicycle and started pumping up into the mountains in quest of my very first deer. As I neared the top of a steep ridge, I pedaled past a real hunting camp, the hunters all decked out in red-and-black checked coats, with four-wheel-drive pickups, and big white wall tents, just like the pictures in the outdoor magazines. Why, when the hunters saw me, pumping up the mountain to go deer hunting, they thought it was the funniest spectacle ever to come their way. And they started yelling at me and laughing and teasing, and carrying on for all they were worth. So I said to myself, "Well, I'll just show you guys. I bet you'll be surprised if I get a deer before you do!"

So I pumped on up the mountain, and just as I came over the top of the last ridge, this nice four-point mule deer buck steps out of the brush and stands there staring at me. I don't know what to do—I'd never shot anything before—and so all at once I just snap off a quick shot at the deer. It drops like a rock! I'm amazed! It was such a difficult shot too, because I was so startled and all shaky and everything—and the rifle was still tied to the handlebars!

Pantomime through looking down at deer, dragging it to bicycle, loading it on bike, and riding down the mountain.

I rush over to the deer to check for bullet holes—but I can't find any. I think maybe the deer is faking it. Then I discover a big chip taken out of one of the antlers—and realize that I hit the deer in the horns so hard that it killed him!

My problem now was how to get the deer home so that my grandmother could dress it out for me. I've noticed that other hunters take their deer home tied to a fender. So I drag the deer over to my bike . . . and lay it across the rear fender. Its head and front hooves drag on one side and the rear hooves drag on the other. I know that's not going to work. Then I remember that I've often carried friends of mine astraddle of the back fender. So I grab the deer and twist it up and around so that it sits astraddle of the fender. I tie each of its front hooves to the handle bars. And I wiggle in between its front legs—I've got the deer's head hanging over my shoulder—and I start pumping toward the brink of that ridge.

Aside to audience: It's a lot harder than you might think, riding a bicycle with a deer on it.

Well, just as my front wheel starts down the steep grade, I hear this strange sound. It's kinda like a—like a—I don't know—kinda like a—a snort!

Pat slowly and fearfully turns and looks at the deer's face.

The deer is blinking its eyes! It panics. First time on a bicycle, I guess.

Well, there's nothing I can do about that now, because already we're flying down the mountain. And the deer is snorting and thrashing about and blowing deer slobber all over me. And I'm trying to steer around rocks and out of ruts and over logs—and just then we pass the hunters camp.

Pat glances at the hunters, grins and waves, as if showing off that he has got a deer before they did.

I can tell they're real surprised to see I got a deer before they did.

The deer and I and the bike continue to fly down the mountain. And then I suddenly realize I've made a terrible mistake—I've forgotten to tie down the deer's hind hooves. And while he's thrashing around, he manages to get his hind hooves onto the pedals! Pretty soon he catches on to pedaling! And he starts to like it!

Aside to audience: You know how fast a deer can run? Well, you haven't seen anything until you've seen a deer on a bike.

We hit the bottom of the mountain, and I throw myself off. The deer and my bike disappear over the horizon.

Later I heard he was in a shootout—with the police—while holding up a liquor store—in Tacoma, Washington—with my rifle!

Commentary

When I first wrote this story for *Field & Stream* magazine back in the seventies, I almost didn't send it in, because I thought I had finally gone over the edge. It seemed so outrageous that I didn't think any editor in his right mind would buy it. In fact, if I hadn't already sold several pieces to the magazine and gotten some fan mail on them, the editor may very well have fired it back to me. Humor writers work with absurdity all the time, but no matter how absurd a story is, it must at least to some small degree remain tethered to reality.

This story originated from an image that popped into my head, that of a deer on a bicycle. I thought the image was funny in and of itself, but how could I build a story around it? Indeed, how was I going to get that deer on the bike?

As I've mentioned somewhere else in this book, writing of all kinds tends to be an exercise in problem solving. I decided to solve the problem by sending "Pat" out on his bicycle to hunt deer. Although that may seem a bit far-fetched, I have met quite a few men and boys over the years who have gone deer hunting on bicycles. And some who even brought deer home on their bikes.

One of the tactical problems with "Deer" is that the "setup" for getting the deer on the bicycle takes so long. There are no really good laughs from the start of the story until the line about the rifle still being tied to the handlebars. And that line wasn't in the original story. I was using "Deer" in a speech at a literary luncheon in a huge department store in Columbus, Ohio. The other speaker was Jane Russell, the movie star, who was out promoting her autobiography. The audience consisted of about eight hundred ladies in white gloves and big hats, every last one of whom had come to listen to Jane, not me. I was a little nervous about what kind of reaction I'd get from all these ladies with my "Deer" story. But it hadn't failed me yet on a promotion tour requiring a dozen or more speeches. I was well into the setup of the story without so much as a snicker from the audience, and worst of all, I still had to shoot the deer. So I shot him. He dropped like a rock, or about the way my speech had dropped so far. And then, grasping at straws, panicking, I blurted out, "The rifle was still tied to the handle bars!" BIG laugh! From then on, I had them. A busboy told me afterwards that the ladies had mascara running down their cheeks and were blowing their noses on their napkins.

After writing the first draft of the story, I decided that I needed an observer in it. So I inserted the hunting camp, even though it stretched the setup out even more without supplying a laugh. The hunting camp works wonderfully well, in that it takes the audience completely by surprise when they come across it again, this time with the deer on the bike.

One of the things that makes the story work is that the people in the audience actually believe it happened, and there is no reason they shouldn't. Everything could have happened just the way it is presented. It certainly isn't hard to believe that a dumb kid might try to bring his deer home just the way it is described. It is stretching it a bit to believe the deer might have regained consciousness on the bike, but still within the realm of possibility. And then, suddenly, the deer gets his hind feet on the pedals and starts to pedal. At that point, we leave the realm of possibility, and members of the audience realize they have been had. They have become part of the joke, part of the comedy, and they love it. Another reason that they surrender their disbelief is that once the deer and Pat go wobbling off on the bicycle they, the audience, are so caught up in laughter they are no longer thinking clearly. Once an audience completely surrenders to absurdity, you have them at your mercy. They are in the grip of what I like to think of as "emotional disorientation." If nothing else, it sounds good. 🚲

***Newton: I get the feeling, Pat , that "The Big Trip"
is a true story. Did you and Retch
actually do this trip?***

We did indeed. It was a great adventure but not something I would
care to repeat. It was a terrible experience, and we barely escaped
with our lives. In other words, it's a perfect subject for humorous
treatment.

"The Big Trip"

When I was very young and the strange wild passion for mountains
was first upon me, I wrote, produced and directed for myself a mag-
nificent, colossal, 3-D, technicolor, wide-screen, stereophonic
fantasy—the fantasy of the Big Trip.

Whenever the jaws of tedium gnawed too harshly on my bones,
I simply turned down the lights on the murk and grind of the world
outside and projected the fantasy on the backsides of my eyeballs,
each of which was equipped with a Silver Screen.

The fantasy was primarily an adventure story set in the vast wilderness of the Selkirk Mountains. It starred You Know Whom, who
bore a striking resemblance to a four-foot-eight-inch Gregory Peck.
The basic plot was that the hero, a pack on his back, hiked far back
into these beautiful mountains, endured great hardships, overcame
terrible obstacles and occasionally even rescued from perilous distress a beautiful red-haired lady. It was strictly a G-rated fantasy (the
R- and X-rated fantasies came later). But I enjoyed it. In fact, with

time, the Big Trip began to gain a strange sort of dominance over my life.

Several times the fantasy prevented my perishing from a loathsome childhood affliction: school. Once, in a seventh-grade English class, I stumbled into a nest of dangling participles. Had I not been able to get my fantasy going in time, those slimy, leechlike creatures would have drained me dry as a puffball in five minutes.

On occasion, Mr. Rumsdale, our seventh-grade English teacher, would unexpectedly break through the thick and buttressed walls of our indifference and start throwing parts of speech in all directions. Several of my friends were knocked silly by flying objects of the preposition, but long before there was any threat to my own cherished ignorance, the old fantasy would carry me to safety. I would be roasting a fresh-caught trout on the rocky shore of some high, distant stream, or maybe just striding along under the sweet weight of a good pack, and it would be morning in the mountains, with the sun rising through the trees.

Mr. Rumsdale once lowered the battering ram he used for a voice and told me that I had better stop this constant dreaming. Otherwise, he predicted, both he and I would probably die as old men in seventh-grade English.

Even by then I knew that the Big Trip, for all its utility as an antidote to boredom, could not endure forever simply as fantasy. One day I would have to turn it into the real thing. I would have to take the Big Trip back into the mountains and face great hardship and overcome terrible obstacles. To that end, I began serving an apprenticeship in the out-of-doors.

I practiced "sleeping out alone" in the backyard, my ears ever alert to the approaching footpad of some hairy terror, until at last I conquered my overpowering fear of the dark and the ghastly things that flourished there. I learned to build fires, using nothing more than a few sticks, a couple of newspapers, and a box-and-a-half of kitchen matches. I studied the art of camp cookery, and soon could serve up a hearty meal of flaming bacon, charred potatoes, three-pound pancakes, and butterscotch pudding with gnat topping. After a longer time, I even taught myself to eat these things. Through practical experience, I learned that it is best not to dry wet boots over a fire with your feet still in them. I learned that some sleeping bags are stuffed with the same filler used in dynamite fuse and that it is best not to let sparks land on one of them, particularly when it is occupied by your body. Thus did the Big Trip shape my life and give meaning even to its failures and disasters.

As I grew older, I went off with friends on numerous lengthy trips into the mountains, thinking each time that perhaps at last I was making the Big Trip. But I never was. These were pleasant, amiable excursions, occasionally distinguished by a crisis or two, but I was always disappointed by the realization that they fell far short of the Big Trip of my aging fantasy. So one day in the summer that I turned seventeen, I decided I would at last, once and for all, plan and execute, or be executed by the Big Trip.

When I announced and elaborated on my plans for the benefit of my mother and stepfather, there was great wailing and gnashing of teeth already well gnashed from my previous and much lesser excursions into the wilderness. From then until the day I left, my mother could scarcely take time out from climbing the walls to make the beds and cook our meals.

The plans were indeed formidable, and in my unsure moments they even caused me to wail and gnash a little. The terrain I planned to cross looked on a topographical map like the scribblings of a mildly demented chimpanzee and spanned a distance of some thirty miles as the crow flies. If the crow walked, it was more like fifty. The area was unmarred by roads or trails. It contained plenty of tracks, though, some of which belonged to grizzlies. And as everyone knows, a grizzly, if he happens along at the right moment, can transform a quiet walk to a privy into a memorable experience.

Preparations for the Big Trip were remarkably simple, since by this time I knew that nothing destroys a Big Trip quicker than a surplus of comforts or a dearth of hardships. And a Big Trip is defined by its hardships.

These hardships, of course, could not be left to mere chance. A number of them had to be prepared in advance and taken along in the pack, so to speak, to be trotted out any time the going got easy. The basic formula for creating hardships is to take no nonessentials and only a few of the essentials.

One of the essentials you leave behind is most of the food. My stock of grub consisted of pancake flour, a slab of bacon, dried fruit, butter, sugar, and salt. For emergency rations, I took a bag of dehydrated chicken noodle soup, enough, it turned out, to feed an army of starving Cossacks for upwards of three weeks.

About the only gear I took was a sleeping bag, a knife and a rifle. I carried along the rifle in case I ran into a grizzly, since my idea of hardships did not include getting eaten by a bear. Although I knew a .32 special couldn't stop a charging grizzly, I took comfort in the notion that I might be able to take the edge off his appetite on his way to the table. In the early days of my fantasy, I had conceived of building a stockade each night as protection against bears, but when you have a grizzly coming for you, no matter how much encouragement and incentive he might offer, it is difficult to get a stockade up in time to do much good. So I was taking the rifle.

At practically the last moment, I decided to take along a companion. In light of the other meticulous preparations for the Big Trip, it seems incongruous now that I should have selected my traveling companion so casually. Retch, as he will be known here, had just moved to town and was probably the only person of my acquaintance who had not heard of the Big Trip. This gap in his knowledge may be the reason that he was the only person I could find who was ready and willing to accompany me on the expedition. Perhaps in my last-minute desperation for companionship I skipped a few details and did not impress upon him the full magnitude of the trip.

"How would you like to go on a camping trip?" I asked him. "Spend a few days hiking around in the mountains, catch some fish, cook out?"

Retch said he thought he would like that. Somehow he got the impression we were going on an extended fishing trip and marshmallow roast. Later, under somewhat harsher circumstances, he was to reveal to me that never in his whole life had he nourished any fantasies about a Big Trip. I was appalled that a human life could be so sterile, so devoid of splendor.

Even by the time my parents were driving us to the jumping-off spot, Retch still did not comprehend the full portent of the Big Trip. My stepfather's funereal air, my mother's quivering lips and my own grim silence, however, began to undermine his confidence.

"It isn't as though we're going to be gone forever," he said, attempting to console my mother. She replied with a low, quavering moan. By the time we disembarked from the car, Retch was convinced that we were going to be gone forever.

As things turned out, he was nearly right.

For two pleasant days, the Big Trip did seem as if it were going to be nothing more than an ordinary camping trip, and therefore not a Big Trip at all. The sky was an impeccable blue, the firewood dry and fragrant, the trout in the lakes fat and hungry, the huckleberries sweet. I could scarcely conceal my disappointment at the good time we were having.

On the third morning I was awakened by a howl of anguish from Retch. "The deer got into our packs and ate everything but the bacon and chicken noodle soup," he yelled.

My heart leaped up. This, finally, was a real hardship.

"Don't worry," I said. "We can always live off the country." Then I looked around. The country didn't seem to be very edible. Perhaps the trip would be harder than even I expected.

Later that same day, we came across what we thought must be fresh grizzly tracks. Concluding that where there are fresh grizzly tracks, there are likely to be fresh grizzlies, we quickened our pace. Near the top of the next mountain, we slowed to a dogtrot, which we maintained for the rest of the day.

That night we camped on a barren ridge without water, and ate fried bacon and soup for supper. The soup, which wasn't much good with water, was even worse without it (the fact that deer had not touched the chicken noodle soup proved to me once and for all that deer are animals of good sense and discriminating taste). After dinner, we sat around the fire picking the bacon out of our teeth with noodles.

"I've got an idea," Retch said.

"What?" I said.

"Let's quit," he said.

Our quitting then would have been like a skydiver's quitting halfway to the ground. "Don't worry," I said. "It will be a lot easier from now on."

Storm clouds were rising in the west when we crawled into our sleeping bags. Soon the heavy black thunderheads were over us. Lightning licked the peak of our mountain a few times and then started walking down the ridge toward us. When it struck close enough to bounce us off the ground, I predicted, breathlessly, "It's going to pass over the top of us. Next time it will strike down below . . ."

By the time I was this far along in my prophecy, it was evident that I didn't have much future as a prophet. It didn't seem as if I even had much future.

When you see lightning hit from a distance, it appears that the bolt zaps into the ground and that's it, but when you are occupying the ground the bolt zaps into, it's not that way at all. First, a terrible bomb goes off and you're inside the bomb, and then streams of fire are going every which way and you're going every which way, and the brush lights up like neon signs in Chinatown, and there are pools of fire on the ground and high voltage sings in the air. Then it's dark again, black, sticky, dark, and the rain hits like a truckful of ice.

The first thing I noticed, upon regaining consciousness, was that I was running to beat hell down the side of the mountain. I was wearing only my shorts. I do not know if I was fully dressed or not when the lightning hit.

Something was bounding like a deer through the brush ahead of me, and I hoped it was a deer and not a grizzly, because I was gaining on it. Then I saw that it was just a pair of white shorts, or reasonably white shorts, also running down the mountain. I yelled at the white shorts that I thought there was a cliff up ahead. The white shorts gave a loud yelp and vanished.

I found Retch sorting and counting his bones at the bottom of a ten-foot drop. He said he might have been hurt worse, but some rocks cushioned his fall.

"You didn't happen to bring an aspirin, did you?" he said.

"No," I said.

"I didn't think so," he said.

While we were draining out sleeping bags (it was raining, remember), I made one last attempt at prophecy.

"Well, Retch," I said, "think of it this way—things just can't get any worse than they are right now."

In the days that followed we were to look back upon that moment as a time of great good fortune and decadent high living.

The driving, ice-cold rain continued throughout the night. The next morning we crawled out of our sleeping bags, stirred around in the mud until we found our clothes, put them on, and with an absolute minimum of jovial banter, spent an unsuccessful hour trying to start a fire. For breakfast we stirred up some chicken noodle soup in muddy water. The muddy water improved the flavor and texture of the soup considerably, and by drinking it through our teeth we could strain out the larger pebbles and even some of the noodles.

On all sides of us, as far as a bloodshot eye could see, was a vast, raging storm of mountains. Our soggy map told us we were ten miles from the end of the nearest trail, more than twenty miles from the nearest road. Retch and I stared at each other across the pile of steaming sticks that represented our aborted effort at fire-building, and I could see a reflection of my own misery and despair swirling in his eyes. "What do we do now?" I thought.

Then I remembered a surefire remedy for predicaments of this sort. It was recommended to me by a fierce old man who knew the mountains well and knew what they can do to a person. "When everything else has failed, there is only one thing to do," he said. "You tough it out."

So that is what we did. We toughed it out. We went down mountains, up mountains, around mountains, lunged over windfalls, through swamps, across rain-swollen streams, and we ate handfuls of chicken noodle mush, and then surged on across more mountains, streams and windfalls. Had we run across a grizzly we would have eaten him raw on the spot and strung his claws for necklaces. There was nothing now, perhaps not even a beautiful red-haired lady in perilous distress, that could have interrupted our relentless march,

And then one day—or was it night?— we walked out of the mountains. There were cars going by on the highway, people zipping comfortably along through their lives at a mile a minute, looking out at us in mild amusement and wondering what muddy, bloody fools were these. We had triumphed over the mountains and over ourselves and over the Big Trip, but nobody knew or cared what we had done. We limped along the road in search of a farmhouse with a phone, our clothes torn, bodies aching, jaws clenched on the bullet, and the last dehydrated chicken noodle soup we would ever eat in our lives still matting our wispy beards.

Then I heard a strange, small sound in the empty air. I glanced over at Retch to see if he heard it too, and he did, and there was this little pained smile on his cracked lips. As we slogged along, the sound grew in volume, swelling up and filling the silence and emptiness until it reached a great thundering crescendo.

It was the sound of applause and cheering—the sound of a standing ovation.

Commentary

"The Big Trip" is one of my favorite stories, because it is pretty much a report of what actually happened and how I thought about the Big Trip. As a young boy, I often fantasized about going off on a great adventure, and I turned that fantasy into reality at age seventeen. The story was written for *Field & Stream*, and I guessed that most of the readers of that magazine would have had their own childhood fantasies of a Big Trip. It's quite possible that the Big Trip fantasy is so widespread among both young men and young women of an adventurous nature that it could be considered as myth. Acting out the myth takes many forms: walking or bicycling across America or around the world, trekking through the Himalayas or climbing Mount Everest, canoeing across the continent, riding the Orient

Express from end to end, and so on. Big Trips have resulted in many fine books. Mark Twain's fantasy of a Big Trip led to one of the greatest works in American literature, *The Adventures of Huckleberry Finn*.

Much of the humor in the story results from contrasting fantasy with reality. There was nothing amusing about the actual Big Trip. "Retch" and I came very close to perishing from injuries, exhaustion and hypothermia. I don't know about Retch, but I learned a great deal about myself on that trip and also something about the strange nature of humor. At one point, we were scaling a near-vertical cliff. Retch, who was just above me, reached a narrow ledge and rolled over on his side to rest. As I pulled myself up to the ledge, Retch and I stared at each other, our heads about six inches apart. Icy rain was pouring down on us, we were both in serious pain from assorted injuries, and before us lay some extremely rugged and dangerous terrain. Believe me, laughter was the furthest thing from my mind, and I know it was from Retch's, as became clear from his matter-of-fact comment to me: "I don't think we're going to make it." For some reason, this calm assessment of our situation struck me as the most hilarious thing I had ever heard, and I burst out laughing so hard I almost fell off the cliff. Retch must surely have thought I had gone mad. Now, not only was he facing the prospect of death on a storm-swept cliff in the middle of nowhere, but he was in the company of a lunatic! Then he too burst out laughing. But what was so funny? Could it be that despair is the ultimate source of comedy, of laughter? I don't know.

I omitted that incident from the story because of the need for brevity and because I thought it would only puzzle most of the readers. I also left out an apparition that occurred near the end of our trek. With the storm long past and the sun now beating down in a last-ditch effort by Mother Nature to finish us off with heat stroke, we emerged from the wilderness on the very tip of a mountain overlooking a valley 5,000 feet below. There in front of us, parked at the end of a logging road, was a beautiful blond lady in a white convertible. She was peacefully contemplating the vista spread out before her.

"What luck!" Retch gasped. "I bet she'll give us a ride down the mountain and back into town. Hey, lady . . . !"

The lady took one horrified look at the two wild and ragged creatures approaching her from behind and took off so fast the rear tires of the car shot gravel a hundred feet straight out into space. As Retch and I limped down the mountain, I contemplated the futility of hope.

I particularly like the ending of this story. Although Retch and I had acted heroically in our adventure, there was no one around to witness our heroism. Only we could know what we had endured and achieved, and it was left to us alone to recognize it as heroic. I suspect that is true of most heroic acts.

"Retch," of course, was not my companion's real name. Because I fictionalized him somewhat, I thought I shouldn't use his real name. The need for brevity in a short-humor piece also seemed to demand that I replace the real name with a fictional one. Use of his real name in the story would have required some description of his personality and character and background, whereas a fictional character has no such previous existence. The substitution of a fictional name for that of a real person in a humor piece also avoids the risk of embarrassing the real person.

This was the first appearance of "Retch" in my stories. I later substituted Retch in many of my accounts of true adventures my friend and I shared, but Retch is not based on anyone in particular. Retch is a bug dumb lazy guy whereas my friend is a trim, bespectacled and accomplished scientist. It is very risky to treat a real person as a comic character. Retch is a character type, a type readers can easily recognize in their own lives, and this recognition is highly useful to the writer of short humor because of the space limits he must work within. Because of his type recognition, readers will "see" the character in vivid detail when they read about him, because they have transferred those details from the real person of a similar type. I know this because readers tell me, "I've got an uncle (or friend or neighbor) exactly like Retch." Or exactly like Rancid Crabtree. Or exactly like Crazy Eddie Muldoon. And of course the character is exactly like Retch or Rancid or Eddie, because they have imposed the image of a real person of the same type onto the character.

I sometimes receive compliments on how well I've described a character, because the reader can actually "see" him in every detail, even though I have never described the character in any detail other than enough to distinguish the type. I have done this deliberately for the most part, at least once I became aware of how the reader supplies most of the visual detail from the clues provided. Suppose, for example, that I gave Rancid bright red hair. Or made him bald. You can see how this would narrow the field of acquaintances the reader would have to select from for transferal of physical character-istics—only men with bright red hair or bald men. Obviously, if you are writing a novel and have unlimited length at your disposal, you would strive for uniqueness in a character. In short humor, how-ever, it is best if you allow the reader to provide that uniqueness.

In the beginning of the piece, it would not have been enough to write that I daydreamed my way through English class. Fortunately, there are such things as dangling participles to treat as slimy, snake-like creatures and objects of the preposition to send flying about. The humor writer must constantly be on the lookout for comic metaphor, which serves the purpose of entertaining the reader while

Newton: *I'm glad you included "Sequences," Pat, because I think it is an absolutely brilliant piece. Of course, I'm only a character you created, so it was easy for you to make me say that.*

I made you say that, Newt, only because it would be immodest of me to say it myself. "Sequences" is one of my favorite pieces, possibly because I received a great deal of favorable comments about it from readers claiming to recognize the problem of sequences in their own undertakings, which indicates that their lives are just as screwed up as my own.

"Sequences"

I have long been a student of sequences, probably because of my upbringing on a farm, and perhaps the larger influence, my association with my stepfather, Hank. My mother remarried several years after my father died, and Hank came to live with us on our Idaho farm. He was a city person, at one time the manager of a minor-league baseball team, who had spent most of his working life in the grocery business. You would expect that someone in the grocery business would know about farming and sequences, but both forever remained a mystery to Hank.

What Hank seemed never able to grasp was that on a farm you simply don't go out and do a piece of work. No, the first thing you do is determine the lengthy sequence of activities necessary even to begin the job. Then you realize that the sequence of preparatory activities is so long you will never get to the intended task. So you go fishing instead. This had been my family's approach to farming for generations, and it worked fine, but Hank could just never get the hang of it.

One day Hank said to me, "Pat, let's take the day off and go fishing up Ruby Crick."

"Sounds good to me," I said. "Let's go."

"Okay. But first we have to fix that hole in the pasture fence. Won't take but twenty minutes."

My shoulders sagged. "Hank," I said, "either we go fishing or we fix the fence. Which is it?"

"Both," he said. "First we fix the fence, then we go fishing. Now go get the wire stretcher and we'll get started."

I saw that it was hopeless. No matter how often I had tried to explain sequences to Hank, he could never grasp their significance. "The wire stretcher's broken," I said.

"Oh, that's right. Well, we'll just run over to the Haversteads and borrow theirs."

"Yeah, but the Malloys borrowed our posthole digger."

"We can swing by the Malloys and pick up our posthole digger on the way back from borrowing the Haversteads' wire stretcher. Then we fix the fence and go fishing. Easy as spit."

"We're out of fence staples, too."

"Is that right? I guess after we borrow the Haversteads' wire stretcher and pick up our posthole digger from the Malloys, we can zip into town and buy some staples at Jergans Hardware, come back, fix the fence, and go fishing."

"But Hank, you promised Sam Jergans you would haul him in a load of hay bales from the Nelsons' the next time you came to town."

"Danged if that ain't what I promised! I got to take Sam the hay when we go for the staples. Otherwise he'll be mad as hops. We'll have to take the truck, but first we better pick up the spare tire that's over at LaRoy's Shop getting fixed. So here's what we'll do. We'll borrow the posthole digger from the Haversteads, pick up our wire stretcher from the Malloys, stop by LaRoy's Shop and get the spare, go over to the Nelsons and load the hay, haul the hay in to Jergans, buy the staples, come home, fix the fence and go fishing. How does that sound?"

"You're getting mixed up, Hank. We borrow the wire stretcher from the Haversteads and then pick up our posthole digger from the Malloys."

"Good leapin' gosh a'mighty, this is gettin' complicated. Now where did we start? I better write it down in the proper . . ."

"Sequence," I said. "We started out to go fishing, but first you wanted to fix that stupid hole in the fence."

It was this early training in sequences that made almost any endeavor in life seem impossible to me. That is why I have just gone fishing instead. I have always enjoyed reading about the great successes so many men and women achieve, and once I even thought I would read a book about how to become a success myself.

"I'm going down to the library to check out a book that tells me how I can become a success," I told my wife, Bun.

"That's a good idea," she said. "I only wish you had read it thirty years ago. Since you're going downtown to the library, will you drop off some clothes at the dry cleaners?"

"Sure."

"I have a coupon for twenty-five percent discount on cleaning. Oh, darn!! I threw the newspaper out. Will you run over to the Smiths and see if they still have theirs? And I told Bev Smith she could have that old trunk in the attic. You can take it over to her when you go, but you'll have to repair the hinge on the attic door first, because otherwise the door will fall off, so when you're down in the basement getting your tool box, I'd like you to—"

"Forget it," I said. "I'm going fishing."

I never did get to read the book on how to become a success. I doubt if I missed much. Once I did go to a seminar on becoming a success, and the speaker said the most important thing was for one to set goals for oneself. That was when I walked out. Any fool can set goals. I've set more goals than a trapper sets traps. I could set half a dozen goals for myself this very minute, without exerting more than a couple of brain cells in the process. The problem is getting to the goals. Every goal has a sequence swirling downward endlessly further and further away from your goal, until you've completely forgotten what the goal was, and your only concern is how to get out of the vortex. It's kind of scary, if you think about it.

I've seen decent, normal persons suddenly come down with ambition and set themselves a goal or two. Then they set off for their goals and you hear a diminishing wail as they're sucked down into the vortex of sequence, and they're never seen again, although sometimes you'll get a postcard from Acapulco. It's much better just to go fishing and forget about success. You'll be happier, take my word for it.

Even fishing can be fraught with sequence, however, and you must be constantly on guard against it. Suppose, for example, Retch Sweeney shows up and asks me to go fishing with him. I say, "Okay," grab rod, reel, tackle box and start out the door.

"What test line you got on that reel?" Retch asks.

"Four-pound."

"Not strong enough for bass. Go put eight-pound on. That would be better."

"Do you want to fish or get sucked into a sequential vortex?" I snap, continuing on out the door.

"What? You got trouble with your drains again? Yeah, let's get outta here before Bun catches us. Four-pound's good enough."

I have never attempted to explain sequences to Retch, but he has an instinct for avoiding them. Somewhere in the spacious recesses of his mind he senses that if I wait to put on eight-pound line before I go fishing, I will never get to the fishing. Maybe there won't be quite enough line to fill the spool. Then I will have to wind the line off the reel spool and back onto the stock spool. Next I will have to find some line to back up the eight-pound line. After that I will have to go to Gary Soucie's *Hook, Line & Sinker* to study the knot for tying two lines together. But then I'll remember I loaned the book to my next-door neighbor, Al Finley, but if I go ask Finley for it, he will want his lawn mower back before Bun has a chance to mow the lawn with it. Thus I will be forced to mow the lawn myself, then return the lawn mower to Finley, get my book back, study the knot, tie the two lines together and wind them on the spool. By then it will be too late to go fishing. It's better to take my chances with four-pound-test.

If you are to achieve any happiness in this world or know a moment's peace, you must learn to view any undertaking not as an isolated event in itself but as a starting point from which you work backwards through endless sequences. The happiest man I ever knew was my old mentor in woodcraft, Rancid Crabtree. Rancid understood the necessity of avoiding sequences. "You can't go chasin' life all over tarnation," he was fond of saying. "You got to sit back and let it come to you. Stay in one place long enough and most everthang'll come by at least once."

It didn't make any sense to me either. But the point is, Rancid was the happiest man I've ever known. Faced with some monumental task or dismal but necessary chore, he didn't sit around whining or cursing his luck. He just squared his shoulders, set his jaw, and said, "This dang nuisance can take care of itself. Let's go fishin'!"

The man knew sequences.

Commentary

Many ideas for humor pieces arise from the simple process of paying attention to your own life and its irritations. For most people, paying attention to their irritations merely makes them more irritable, but it can be profitable for the writer. "Hey!" the writer says to himself. "This really irritates the heck out of me. Great! I bet I can get a piece out of this." Such was the case with "Sequences." I simply noticed the process I go through whenever I undertake almost any project, no matter how simple.

This idea could have been directed toward many different kinds of audiences, because sequences are an inescapable form of behavior in all walks of life. In this case, I happened to be writing for an audience of outdoor enthusiasts, and so I slanted the idea to the outdoors through use of the fishing refrain. I could just as easily have slanted it to an audience of teachers, housewives, mechanics, psychologists or whomever.

The sequence idea could have been developed in many different ways. I chose to illustrate it with the Hank/fence scenario, because that seemed to have better comic possibilities. I like to bring characters in whenever possible, particularly when writing about an abstraction like sequences, and Hank seemed perfect to cast for the part of a man who doesn't understand them.

People tend to think of their behavior and situations as unique to themselves, but the writer, at least the humor writer, should think of his behavior and situation as universal. I received such a huge response from readers of "Sequences" that it became evident to me that most of humanity must be swirling around in the vortex of one sequence or another.

Among the great rewards of writing—and money is seldom one of them—is to hear your readers exclaim, "Oh, that is so true!" Because the average person, the normal person, doesn't have any particular reason to pay attention to the peculiarities of his behavior, he gets this little charge of delight when a writer points out something he recognizes as his own but never really noticed before. This is the Recognition Factor at work.

One day when we were moving from our old house to a newer old house, my wife came out of the bathroom carrying a couple of towels. "I put up these towels for curtains as a temporary measure," she said. "That was fifteen years ago!" It instantly occurred to me that most people probably have all kinds of temporary measures that become permanent. Here was a Recognition Factor. So I wrote a humor piece about how most of life tends to be based upon temporary measures. Readers agreed in significant numbers. It occurred to me one day that I am never without worries. As soon as one worry vanishes, I replace it with another—a Recognition Factor. This provided the idea for a story titled "The Worry Box." Every person has in his head a box of a certain fixed size to contain his worries. Some people have big worry boxes and other have small worry boxes, but whatever the size, the box is always full. Usually the box is filled with a bunch of little worries and sometimes with one big worry. If you see a grizzly bear coming down the trail toward you (outdoor slant), you instantly toss out all the little worries from your worry box and fill it with one big worry—GRIZZLY!

Once I had the idea for it, "Sequences" was a fairly easy story to write. I had only to invent some examples of sequences at work, and to make them as humorous as I could. I would like to see "Sequences" in my one-man stage show, but can't. My actor can never remember the sequences! As a matter of fact, I can't either. 🚲

Newton: Oh, great! I see you have included the piece in which I am a character—"As the Ear Is Bent."

Yes, Newton, I knew you would be pleased. As you can see, however, you don't get any lines of your own. And there's good reason for that. I had to place great trust in the imagination of the reader to create most of the "story" from the clues provided.

"As the Ear Is Bent"

Persons newly introduced to hunting, fishing and camping can often learn a great deal from paying close attention to the comments of their more experienced companions, particularly those who have entered into geezerhood. What follows is an example of the kind of geezer comments to which a beginning outdoorsman should be particularly alert, if he is to profit from the wisdom of his more experienced companion.

"Since this is your first camping trip, Newton, I'm gonna let you have the side of the tent with a nice view of the stars."

"Sasquatch? Ain't no such thing as a Sasquatch, Newton. You hear all sorts of weird sounds like that outside a tent at night. You go check it out while I look for my glasses."

"I'll go over there on the other side of the crick and chop some firewood, Newton, while you light my old gas lantern."

"Okay, Newton, here's a little problem I thought up to test your sense of direction. Got any idea where we left the car?"

"Raisins in the hash? You think I put raisins in the hash, Newton? Yep, that's what they are, raisins. No, they don't have wings! Now stop digging at your food and eat!"

"Well, I'd better go over across the crick and chop some more firewood while you light the lantern again. By the way, and please don't take offense at this, Newton, but I think you look a whole lot better without that scraggly beard."

"Here's another little test of your woodsmanship, Newton. Bet you don't know the way back to camp."

"This ain't no time to be checking to see what side of the tree the moss is growing on, Newton. Moss don't care one iota whether you live or die out here."

"It's not a good idea to suddenly shout out 'Sasquatch!' Newton, even if there ain't no such thing. When you're lost in the woods, just about anything can set off a panic. You got to remember that, son. One good thing, though, I can see camp from up here in the tree."

"Any fool can pound in tent pegs with a hatchet, Newton, but it takes skill to perform that task with the outdoorsman's basic tool — the flat rock! Let me demonstrate."

"What you saw me perform there, Newton, is known technically as the 'Crouch Hop!' Did you notice how I clasped my flattened thumb between my thighs before bounding about camp? You can make up your own chant, but 'Yi Yi Yi!' is one of my favorites, particularly when ladies and children are present."

"I'm sorry about your head, Newton. I hadn't realized you'd decorated your lucky hunting hat with fur and bear claws. Looked to me like it had sprung out of a tree and latched onto your scalp. So that's when I grabbed up the stick."

"I don't care what miners used to do, Newton, we ain't bringing no canary into the tent. If you're going to be so dang fussy, you can do the cooking."

"Time for you to light the lantern again, Newton. I'll be over across the crick. Oh, I should mention that I think you look a whole lot better without that squirrelly little mustache. You bet!"

"That was a nice punt, Newton. I just wish you'd aimed the lantern toward the crick instead of the tent. Come to think of it, of what use are eyebrows, really? Seems to me a fella is just as well off without 'em."

"You see, Newton, a lean-to made out of sticks and a few cedar boughs can make a nice, comfortable shelter. If you don't figure out where we left the car pretty soon, we might think about putting up a few pictures. Ha! Seriously, though, you think real hard about where we parked the car, because I'm not going to give you the answer."

"You what? You found the car, Newton? Now, wasn't it right where I parked it? So there you go. What have I been telling you? Not to worry when you're out with the Old Geeze, huh?"

"You'd like to snack on some raisins while you're driving home? What makes you think we brought along any raisins, Newton?"

"Why thanks for saying that, Newton. It's nice to hear that after this little outing with me, you feel much better equipped to survive your next camping trip."

Commentary

This is a form of short humor that I use fairly often. I think of it as an advice column. Sometimes I will give the reader "advice" on how to buy a boat, get started in bass fishing, prepare for a first date, etc. This piece is a little different. Here the Old Geezer is giving the advice to young Newton while on a camping trip. The camping trip itself is deliberately obscured in the sense that the author of the piece is not reporting about it directly to the reader. Almost everything that happens on the trip must be interpreted from the Old Geezer's offhand comments. The comic idea operating here is that the Geezer has his own agenda, which consists mostly of taking advantage of Newton and concealing his own incompetence as an outdoorsman.

Although it seems simple enough once it's done, the hardest part of writing a humor piece like this is setting up the situation with that first paragraph. Although the sole purpose of the story is to amuse, a pretense is made of having the exercise serve a practical purpose. The advice or instructional column is a form that is used over and over in short humor.

This column was written for *Outdoor Life,* where the readers will have no trouble identifying with Newton when it comes to lighting an old gas lantern—the Recognition Factor in operation.

***Newton: Whoa! What's going on here, Pat? "Wild
Life in a Room with a View" looks like a
straight piece, a regular article.***

It is, Newt. Back in the days when I wrote mostly factual articles, I
soon learned that humor could greatly enhance the salability of the
piece. I doubt very much that without the inclusion of the humorous anecdotes that this story would ever have sold to *Sports Illustrated*.

"Wild Life in a Room with a View"

Each June, about the time most people think of vacations and many
begin moving to the seashore, a few hundred strangely assorted
Americans head for the high mountains and great forests of the land.
Their stated purpose is to help prevent forest fires. But what they
really have in mind is the ultimate get-away-from-it-all, an escape
into the blissful solitude of a delightful little wilderness penthouse —
a U.S. Forest Service lookout station. Helping to prevent forest fires
is merely the price they must pay for their room with a view. Early
each September, out they come again, and from their stories one
wonders if the solitude is all that blissful, the price that mere, or the
penthouse that delightful; there are, it seems, a few trials and even
some tribulations.

To begin with, the living quarters are a bit cramped — twelve to
fourteen feet square — and are nestled atop towers anywhere from
ten to one-hundred feet high. Fuel, food, water and all other supplies needed to sustain an easy life must be toted by hand up the
stairs, which can seem interminable. The sanitary facility is fifty

yards off in the bushes, and the nearest source of water may be a mile or more down the mountain. During storms the higher towers have a tendency to sway sickeningly, lightning strikes with unmonotonous regularity a few feet from where the lookout is sitting (or kneeling) and balls of weird blue "fire" from time to time sizzle about the place like water on a hot skillet. The lookouts are assaulted by insects, besieged by beasts, seared by the sun, chased by forest fires and perhaps worst of all, tortured incessantly by the monstrous silence. This is to say nothing of the work; but, as one lookout suggests, the work consists largely of being there.

The experience of the Forest Service suggests that no particular kind of individual is ideally suited to life in a tower suite, and the recruits who show up for training early each summer prove to be a strangely mixed lot: prim lady schoolteachers, college professors, ministers' wives, loggers, vacationing businessmen, farmers, grandmothers, coeds, honeymooners, old marrieds, beauty queens, students, female truck drivers, ex-marines and cookie-baking housewives; in short, just about anyone who can shake off the fetters of routine life for three months.

Newlyweds long ago discovered that lookout towers make private places for honeymoons, and each forest usually has at least one couple launching its marriage atop a peak. Rangers, reluctant marriage counselors that they are, generally avoid pointing out to the couples that if a marriage can survive a summer in a lookout tower it can survive almost anything. Their fervent hope is that the rocks the marriage may be headed for won't be those at the foot of the tower. Familiarity may or may not breed contempt, but there is no doubt that the tiny cabins breed profuse amounts of familiarity. Paul Wilson, dispatcher for the Coeur d'Alene (Idaho) National Forest, recalls one couple that stopped speaking to each other fifteen minutes after being moved into their cabin. "Right then I knew it was going to be a long, hard season," says Paul. "And it was, for all concerned."

But whatever small apprehensions the honeymooners may create for the rangers, newlyweds almost always turn out to be highly competent and dedicated fire lookouts, not to mention a source of considerable humor. Visitors to one of these bridal towers listened in fascination recently as a blue-jeaned bride gave her impressions about honeymooning on a lookout platform, "One thing I've noticed is that the days seem so long and the nights so short!" Her stricken husband hastened to explain that this was because the tower was the highest point in the mountains and was, consequently, the first thing the sun's rays touched in the morning and the last in the evening. The nights actually were shorter.

The Forest Service likes to man its towers with married couples whenever possible. For one thing, the lookouts are not so lonely; they can break the monotony by making either love or war. For another, the government gets two pairs of eyes for the price of one. The husband is paid for the five weekdays and the wife for Saturday and Sunday. In practice, of course, the husband and wife are both in the tower most of the time and are therefore both watching for fires most of the time. As one official points out, "There just isn't that much else to do."

Sometimes the lookouts are single women. Last summer twenty-three of the two hundred and thirty-three stations in the Northern Region were operated by female fire spotters. The consensus among rangers is that they do an excellent job, frequently surpassing the men. "They are more observant," says a ranger. "They hold their interest well in what can be a monotonous job, and they keep meticulous records. They also keep their quarters in much better condition." One girl, a coed from Idaho Sate University "who didn't know a meadow bottom from a ridge top," was assigned to an observation cab atop a one-hundred-foot steel tower overlooking a vast area of the Nez Perce National Forest. Not only did she adapt quickly and well to this awesome place of work, but within two weeks she had memorized the names of every ridge and water drainage in sight. Other women operate the complex network of stations that serve as communications centers for the Forest Service and various other state and federal agencies.

Although men are preferred in stations where smoke chasing and fire fighting may be a part of the duties, the Lava Butte station in the Deschutes National Forest in Oregon was once manned by a lady who did all her own fire fighting. Having formerly worked on a tugboat, she was known, naturally as "Tugboat Annie." She further endeared herself to the foresters by smoking cigarettes in a long, elegant holder, which she would use to point out various features of the landscape to any occasional visitors.

Many of the women return year after year. Mrs. Carol Sopher, the only woman lookout in the Bitterroot National Forest of Montana last year, has spent seventeen summers in fire towers, and Dorothy Taylor, a former schoolteacher, has worked for nearly twenty years in Montana's Lolo National Forest.

Not only are the rangers pleased to see the ladies return, but so are the squirrels and chipmunks that live in the rocks around the stations, for they receive a lot of maternal care. One lady fire watcher baked sugar cookies every day to feed to the golden-mantled squirrels around her station, and by summer's end she could bring them running by calling, "Here, kitty, kitty, kitty!" Another lady lookout fed her chipmunks hotcakes daily. "By the end of summer," says a ranger, "they were so fat they looked like marmots."

Larger wild animals, although seldom dangerous, contribute their full share to the tribulations of the lookouts. Porcupines are fond of the salt in rubber and will eat the tires, and even the fan belts, off a lookout's automobile. Mountain goats like to gather in the middle of the night for a playful romp on the catwalk that surround the lookout's sleeping quarters. The goats so successfully upset the nights of one lookout that he kept falling asleep during working hours, an offense which the Forest Service ranks about equal to that of the Army sentry who dozes at his post. He finally built a barricade to keep the goats off the tower stairs.

Many of the lookouts are from large cities and at first have some difficulty identifying their wild animals. A lookout once radioed in that he had a coyote around his tower. For several days he entertained the boys back at the ranger station with descriptions of the antics of this friendly and daring animal. When he told one day of the coyote's trying to claw its way into the cabin, the rangers decided they had better have a look at the critter. It turned out to be a bear. Another lookout, obviously nervous, reported, "Big, hairy beasts are ganging up around the foot of my tower." He went outside for another look, and quickly returned to the radio. "Now they're coming up the stairs!" he shouted. The local ranger leaped into his four-wheel drive and flailed it all the way to the tower, his imagination conjuring up the wildest of Alfred Hitchcock scenes. The troublemakers turned out to be a family of pack rats.

Most of the lookouts develop their own methods for dealing with animals that make nuisances of themselves, as did the lady who observed a large bear ascending her tower stairs. When the bear did not heed her vocal threats, she went inside, heated a pot of water and dumped it on him. He was not seen in the neighborhood again. This procedure, through it may seem absurdly domestic and urban, is now the approved procedure for discouraging bears that like to climb towers.

Occasionally a bear will threaten a lookout with bodily harm, but only when the lookout is accompanied by a loyal and courageous dog and armed with much good advice is he likely to be in danger. Doug McFarland, a young lookout in the Primitive Area of Idaho, was clearing a trail during one wet period when the fire danger was low. He was accompanied by his trusty Irish setter and had been told that if he saw a large bear preparing to mount an attack the best thing to do was to give a loud whoop. A couple of miles down the trail from his tower McFarland noticed the first sign of a bear: the silent, reddish blur of his dog passing him, fleeing in the opposite direction. Shortly thereafter the bear emerged from the brush, cleared the field of battle by ushering her twin cubs up a nearby tree and charged. Quickly recalling the good advice, McFarland let out a loud whoop. The bear rushed on. McFarland whooped again. Still the bear didn't stop. "My third whoop was entirely involuntary," McFarland recalls, "but apparently I at last had whooped authentically." The bear skidded to a stop a few feet away and returned reluctantly to her cubs. Shakily, McFarland made his way back to the lookout tower, where his dog awaited him under the bed.

There are other fire watching hazards. The safest place to be during a lightning storm, rangers like to explain as they sit comfortably in their office swivel chairs, is a lookout tower. This, they claim, is because the towers are decorated with such a formidable mass of lightning rods that it is virtually impossible to be electrocuted there (rangers do not entertain the possibility of a person's being frightened to death). When lightning does strike a tower the lookout is, of course, sitting at the point of impact. To fully appreciate the stimulating effect of this, you must recall the last time that you saw a great ragged bolt of lightning split the sky and then counted— "one thousand one, one thousand two . . ." until the sound of thunder finally arrived. In a lookout tower struck by lightning the thunder and flash are simultaneous, creating an effect that is presumably like that of sitting inside an exploding bomb.

The rangers consider the first lightning storm as the qualifying exam for their new lookouts. "Up to then they're amateurs," says one forester. "After it, they're pros." Last summer a new lookout became a pro his first night on the job. His tower was struck nine times. Asked if he would like a few days off to pull himself together, the lookout said no, he would stick to his post—an obvious case of shell shock.

In addition to lightning rods, the Forest Service supplies the lookout with a chair that has a glass insulator on the bottom of each leg. If the lookout sits in the chair, first making sure that it is not situated between two pieces of metal—electricity might arc between them—and if he avoids touching the radio or telephone, puts in his earplugs and does not leap off the tower, he has an excellent chance of surviving strike after strike with nothing more serious than jangling nerves, psychedelic eyeballs and recurrent nightmares.

Less spectacular than lightning but much more haunting are the weird balls of blue fire that sometimes are seen dancing about lookout stations during electrical storms. This phenomenon is called "St. Elmo's fire" and is caused by harmless static electricity.

Forest fires seldom endanger lookouts, and if a fire should threaten a station there usually is ample time to beat a retreat. But not always. The Sundance fire in Idaho in the summer of 1967 proved an exception for eighteen-year-old Randy Langston. Stationed on 7,264-foot Roman Nose Peak, Randy had been keeping an eye on the fire, which had been burning fitfully for several weeks. On the evening of September 1, the fire was about fifteen miles and a mountain range away from the Roman Nose lookout. Then, in a matter of hours, a sixty-mph wind whipped the Sundance blaze into one of the worst in Idaho's smoky history. In a single day the fire made a run of twenty-one miles, eventually threatening towns, farms and homes along a thirty-mile front. At its worst it burned one square mile of mature timber every three minutes, and its smoke column rose to a height of 45,000 feet. Trapped in the middle of this inferno, Randy continued to make his radio reports until it became evident that the fire was going to sweep right over his tower. He was ordered to take his radio and try to find shelter in the rocks below the station. The young lookout scrambled down to a rock slide, where he spent the night surrounded by a violent fire storm. The following morning a helicopter picked him up and flew him to safety. He was a bit shaken, but unsinged.

And the lookout tower? Well, it survived, too. It stands now as a lonely and useless sentinel over 51,000 charred acres that made up one of the most beautiful forest areas in Idaho.

The lookout begins his summer of tranquillity by attending a week-long fireguard training school conducted by each national forest. There he learns the various methods of spotting and fighting fires. After completing his training he usually moves straight into the lookout station he has been assigned to. Most of the stations now have rough roads leading to them, but a few can be reached only by horse, helicopter or on foot. In the early days of lookout stations, the lookout went "in" and stayed "in" for the season, but now he can usually have a day or two in town each week while a substitute takes his place. In the case of a married couple, the wife can hop in the car and drive to town for a loaf of bread or a divorce.

The first weeks at the station may be spent clearing trails, stringing telephone wires, maintaining roads or giving the tower a new coat of paint. Daily weather reports are also made. Once the fire season arrives, however, which is usually in early June, lookouts concentrate on their primary job and every twenty minutes must make a systematic check of the area protected by their stations. After a week or so the twenty-minute check is all but forgotten, because the lookout is in the habit of looking. Indeed, he can hardly stop looking.

"After a while they just look around all the time," a ranger explains. "You can't hold a decent conversation with them because their heads are constantly turning this way and that. They look like owls."

Competition between lookouts becomes fierce. Not only do they check their own territory but each other's, and it is a major triumph to spot an unreported "smoke" in the other fellow's range. Working hours as such become purely academic, and lookouts will make a habit of getting up in the middle of the night to make sure a fire has not sneaked into their area under cover of darkness. Needless to say, the Forest Service subtly encourages this spirit of friendly competition.

New lookouts at first have some trouble identifying smokes. They will report patches of fog, clouds, dust and, at night, even the lights from each other's stations. But by the time the fire season arrives they have become experienced enough to know smoke when they see it. Still, they tend to be jumpy and do not take any chances. Last summer, during the height of the Idaho fire season, a lookout reported smoke he had just spotted. As it happened, a plane loaded with retardant to be dumped on another fire was just clearing the runway. It was ordered to the new blaze instead. Fortunately, the pilots are required to make a dry run over each suspected site before they bomb. Down below, the pilot could see a logging crew staring nervously up at him as he roared over at treetop level. The smoke was a plume of blue exhaust fumes caused by starting a bulldozer.

Base pay for lookouts ranges from $2.15 to $2.40 an hour. They also may earn a monthly increment of from fifteen percent to twenty-five percent of their base pay by working an additional twenty-eight hours a week. They must furnish all of their own provisions, but the room—and the view—is free.

In recent years most of the stations have been "modernized," which means that wood-burning stoves have been replaced with propane combination stove-refrigerator units. If the lookout's stove burns wood, he must split it himself, regulations requiring that he keep a two-week supply on hand at all times. Stations unequipped with propane also have no means of refrigeration, thus depriving the lookout of the luxury of perishable foods and cool drinks (one young lookout's parents eased—or perhaps ruined—their son's summer on his own by flying their private plane over his station every couple of days and parachuting him a quart of ice cream). The only time any of the lookouts have running water is if they should break into a sprint while carrying it up from the nearest spring.

The Forest Service is quite concerned that its lookouts not go overboard with the "roughing it" concept. The lookouts are representatives of the U.S. Government, the rangers point out, and are expected to create a favorable impression. There is no telling when one of the taxpayers may show up for an impromptu visit, regardless of where the station is located, and he is not to find empty food cans moldering on the floor or shorts and bra hung up to dry on the firefinder. After each sprinkling of rain, the windows—all forty or so panes—are to be polished spotlessly clean. Ledges must be dusted daily and the floors and steps—no matter how many of them—must be swept. The grounds are to be kept free of clutter by burning or burying debris.

Lookout stations, once merely functional, are now becoming tourist attractions of sorts. They make excellent destinations for hiking clubs. If he gets careless, a lookout who has not seen another human in a month could find himself kicking cans under his bunk, dusting the table with the T-shirt he has just snatched from the firefinder and hastily setting his abode in acceptable U.S. representative-type order as thirty-seven members of the Hill Hoppers Outing Club ascend his stairs. The government is even publishing little pamphlets describing lookout stations that the public might like to visit.

The Forest Service currently operates approximately one thousand lookout stations throughout the country during the fire season. The number has decreased by several hundred during the last few years as many areas changed from a detection system relying almost entirely on fixed ground lookouts to one employing a few key ground stations supplemented by aircraft patrol. But there is no thought that the ground stations can ever be completely abandoned. Thus, he who would escape for three whole months the grit and grind of people-glutted cities to spend the summer on a Forest Service lookout station will have the opportunity. There is no need to rush. Simply obtain from your local post office and fill out several copies of Application for Federal Employment, Standard Form 57, and mail them to the ranger district in the national forest of your choice. The Forest Service usually hires its lookouts during January, but a few replacements are taken on as late as May.

So just imagine it. There you are, relaxing on the tower steps as the sun sinks slowly in the west and the darkness rises out of the pine-clad depths of the mountains, finally to embrace this little penthouse, your room with a view. Touched by the last lingering rays of the sun, the tower glows like the first star of evening in the great blue bowl of the sky. Peace. Beauty. Somewhere off down the mountain a coyote wails. Then your keen, woodsman-type ear picks up a faint sound. It is the porcupines gnawing on your car tires. From the edge of an alpine grove you glimpse a herd of mountain goats approaching your tower stairs. The breeze is picking up, the tower is beginning to sway, and rising in the south, blotting out the stars, is a massive thunderhead. It is at times like this that you truly rejoice in your solitude; there is no one around to hear you cry.

Commentary

This is one of the last "straight" articles I wrote before switching almost exclusively to short-humor pieces. Even though it is a factual piece, its overall tone tends to be humorous, which perhaps foreshadowed the direction I was soon to take.

The odd thing about the article is how I came up with the idea for it. I was teaching a class in magazine article writing, and more or less off the top of my head decided to take students through the process of coming up with an idea for an article.

"Let's take a topic at random," I said. I looked out the classroom window and saw some trees.

"How about trees?" I said. "But that's way too broad. Let's narrow the topic down to something related to trees. Let's say, uh, the U. S. Forest Service.

"Still too broad. Let's narrow the topic down to some part of the Forest Service, say, fire lookout towers.

"But fire lookout towers are things. People are always more interesting than things. So let's write about the people who staff the towers.

"Okay, now we have our topic but we still don't have an idea for the article. Ideas typically show a relationship between two or more things. It could be a causal relationship, A causes B. Then there is the best of a thing, worst of a thing, first, last, biggest, smallest, etc. Those ideas are pretty standard in article writing but I don't think they would work here.

"Another good idea is illusion versus reality. For example, we could say that the people who staff the lookout towers have the illusion that the job will be a three-month summer vacations BUT the reality is that it is hard, boring and even dangerous work.

"So now we have our article idea. Can we make it interesting? There must be plenty of highly entertaining anecdotes about people sitting atop towers all summer long in the national forests. They must have problems with wild animals, lightning, forest fires, the primitive facilities. Most of these anecdotes should be easy to obtain by interviewing a few Forest Service rangers.

"Now, what's the 'spread' for the article. By spread, I mean how can we spread the interest in this article to readers all over the country, rather than limiting it just to the Pacific Northwest. The article should be entertaining because of all the anecdotes, but we should also tie each reader to the article in some way. We should give each reader the opportunity to think of himself or herself as potentially being a candidate for one of the lookout jobs, It doesn't make any difference whether the person lives in Kansas or Montana or Pittsburgh, anyone can apply. So we'll include in the article some information about how to go about getting a lookout job.

"We have the 'spread' for a national article; now we need a national magazine. Our chances of selling this article to a national magazine are better if the editors view it as something offbeat. It should strike the editors as something totally new and different for them to run, but still appropriate to the usual content of the magazine. What kind of magazine meets that qualification? How about *Sports Illustrated*? It runs articles almost entirely about sports, so an article about Forest Service fire lookouts would certainly be offbeat for SI.

"But maybe too offbeat. Can we come up with a slant that would allow the article to fit into the normal context of *Sports Illustrated*? Well, the magazine does occasionally run articles on nature, wildlife and outdoor sports. Forests are certainly nature, and we'll also have plenty of wildlife in the article. So there's our slant for *Sports Illustrated*.

"Now, we need one last thing—the editorial concept. We need to come up with a phrase that will make the editor instantly visualize the article in his magazine. How about something like, 'Wild Life in a Room with a View?" (Editorial concepts often becomes the titles for articles, as happened in this case.)

It took me most of the class period to run through the process for developing a hypothetical magazine article idea. Then it suddenly occurred to me that the idea didn't have to be hypothetical. I sent a query letter off to *Sports Illustrated* that very day and almost immediately received an assignment to do the article.

In writing the article, I emphasized the humorous aspects of it because I viewed the reader interest to be primarily one of entertainment as opposed to, say, information the reader could somehow put to use, as in a how-to piece. Nevertheless, as you will see in reading the article, I did put in a little "how-to" in order to make a connection between the reader and the topic. At least for an instant, I wanted the reader to think, "Hey, I might do this, become a lookout over the summer. I wonder how I should apply?" And so I tell him how to apply, what training he will get, what his duties will be, etc., even though down deep both he and I know he will never in his entire life spend one minute in a fire lookout tower. The basic purpose of the article was to amuse and entertain, not inform. The editors at *Sports Illustrated* clearly saw it the same way I did, and illustrated the piece with cartoons rather than photographs.

Note that the illusion/reality idea for the article is expressed in the lead: the candidates for the lookout jobs start with the illusion that a summer on a fire tower will make a great vacation but the reality turns out to be something totally different.

The second paragraph is still part of the lead. It summarizes all the disasters that can befall the lookouts. This is a "hook." It hooks the readers into continuing with the article so that they can find out the details about the problems briefly mentioned in this paragraph. The rest of the article is devoted to satisfying the curiosity aroused in these two lead paragraphs.

After being published in *Sports Illustrated*, the article was abridged and reprinted in *Reader's Digest*, the first appearance of my work in that magazine.

"Wild Life in a Room with a View" could have been slanted to any number of magazines. Because so many women staffed lookout towers, many of the women's magazines would have made good markets. It would have worked for any of the major outdoor/nature magazines, *Audubon* being a particularly good one for this article. It would have been perfect for almost any general-interest magazine, such as *Saturday Evening Post, Smithsonian,* or for that matter *Reader's Digest.*

In a market report for *The Writer* magazine, the articles editor I worked with at *Sports Illustrated* later used "Wild Life" as an example of the kind of freelance piece SI might buy. Interestingly, he mentioned many of the points I had listed in my class demonstration of how to arrive at an idea for an article. The article, he said, was offbeat, well researched, humorous, well written, slanted to SI's readership and so on. Having made an impression on the editors of SI, I probably could have continued doing freelance articles for them for many years. Instead, I strayed off into the swamp of comedy and haven't yet found the way out. 🚲

Newton: *Gee, Pat, I don't know about this next story, "The Night the Bear Ate Goombaw." It seems as if Mr. Muldoon is already having a terrible time, and then you haul him up into the mountains and make matters even worse for him. Is that funny?*

Yes, Newt, I think it is. Don't ask me why, but I think there is far greater potential for comedy in adding to the misery of the down-and-outer than there is in inserting a little misery into the comfortable life of the rich playboy. A reasonable person would think it should be the other way around, but a reasonable person, of course, wouldn't be a humor writer in the first place.

"The Night the Bear Ate Goombaw"

There was so much confusion over the incident anyway that I don't want to add to it by getting the sequences mixed up. First of all — and I remember this clearly — it was the summer after Crazy Eddie Muldoon and I had been sprung from third grade at Delmore Blight Grade School. The Muldoons' only good milk cow died that summer, shortly after the weasel got in their chicken house and killed most of the laying hens. This was just before the fertilizer company Mr. Muldoon worked for went bankrupt, and he lost his job. The engine on his tractor blew up a week later, so he couldn't harvest his crops, which were all pretty much dried up from the drought anyway.

Then Mr. Muldoon fell in the pit trap that Crazy Eddie and I had dug to capture wild animals. Our plan was to train the wild animals and then put on shows to earn a little extra money for the family. But Mr. Muldoon fell in the trap, and afterwards made us shovel all the dirt back into it. The only wild animal we had trapped was a skunk, and when Mr. Muldoon fell in on top of it, he terrified the poor creature practically to death. Neither Mr. Muldoon nor the skunk was hurt much, but the skunk managed to escape during all the excitement. So there went our wild-animal show. This occurred about midsummer, as I recall, about the time Mr. Muldoon's nerves got so bad that old Doc Hicks told him to stop drinking coffee, which apparently was what had brought on his nervous condition.

For the rest of the summer, Mr. Muldoon gave off a faint, gradually fading odor of skunk. Unless he got wet. Then the odor reconstituted itself to approximately its original power, which placed a major restraint on the Muldoons' social life, meager as that was. Fortunately, Mr. Muldoon didn't get wet that often, mainly because of the drought that had killed off his crops. As Mrs. Muldoon was fond of saying, every cloud has a silver lining.

So far it had been a fairly typical summer for Mr. Muldoon, but he claimed to be worried about a premonition that his luck was about to turn bad. Then Eddie's grandmother, Mrs. Muldoon's mother, showed up for a visit.

"I knew it!" Mr. Muldoon told a neighbor. "I knew something like this was about to happen. I must be psychic."

After I got to know Eddie's grandmother a little better, I could see why Mr. Muldoon regarded her visit as a stroke of bad luck. She immediately assumed command of the family and began to boss everyone around, including me. Nevertheless, I doubted that Mr. Muldoon was actually psychic, because otherwise he would never have come up with the idea of the camping trip.

"I'm worried about Pa," Eddie said one morning as we sat on his back porch. "He's not been hisself lately."

"Who's he been?" I asked, somewhat startled, although I regarded Mr. Muldoon as one of the oddest persons I knew.

"Pa's just started acting weird, that's all. You know what crazy idea he came up with this morning? He says we all gotta go on a camping trip up in the mountains and pick huckleberries. He says we can sell any extra huckleberries we get for cash. But Pa don't know anything about camping. We don't even have any camping stuff. Ain't that strange?"

"Yeah," I said. "Say, Eddie, you don't suppose your pa . . . uh . . . your pa . . ." I tried to think of a delicate way to phrase it.

"What?" Eddie said.

"Uh, you don't suppose your pa, uh, would let me go on the camping trip too, do you?"

When Eddie put the question to his father Mr. Muldoon tried to conceal his affection for me beneath a malevolent frown. "Oh, all right," he growled at me. "But no mischief. That means no knives, no hatchets, no matches, no slingshots and *no shovels*! Understood?"

Eddie and I laughed. It was good to see his father in a humorous mood once again.

I rushed home and asked my mother if I could go camping with the Muldoons. "You'd be away from home a whole week?" she said. "I'll have to think about that. Okay, you can go."

I quickly packed my hatchet, knife, and slingshot, along with edibles mom gave me to contribute to the Muldoon grub box. The one major item I lacked was a sleeping bag. "I'll just make a bedroll out of some blankets off my bed," I informed my mother.

"You most certainly won't," she informed me. "You'll use the coat."

"Ah, gee, ma, the coat's so stupid. Mr. Muldoon will tease me all during the trip if I have to use that stupid coat for a sleeping bag."

The coat in question was a tattered, dog-chewed old fur of indeterminate species that my grandmother had acquired during a brief period of family wealth in the previous century. It had been given to me as a "sleeping bag" for my frequent but always aborted attempts at sleeping out alone in the yard. For all its hideous appearance, it was warm and cozy, and covered my nine-year-old body nicely from end to end. Still, I knew the Muldoons would laugh themselves silly when they saw me bed down in a woman's fur coat. My only hope of retaining a shred of dignity, not to mention my carefully nursed macho image, was to slip into it after they had all gone to sleep. I stuffed the coat into a gunnysack, concealing it under the one threadbare blanket my mother reluctantly issued me.

The day of the big camping trip dawned bright and clear, a common ruse of Mother Nature to lure unsuspecting souls out into the wild. The five of us piled into the ancient Muldoon sedan and set off for the mountains, most of our camping gear, such as it was, balanced precariously atop the car. It was wrapped in a huge hay tarp, which was to serve as our tent. "Ain't had a drop of rain in three months," Mr. Muldoon had said. "Probably won't need the tarp." This statement would later be recalled and admitted as evidence in the case against Mr. Muldoon's being psychic.

"How you doin' back there, Goombaw?" Mr. Muldoon said to Eddie's grandmother. For some reason, everyone called her Goombaw.

"How you think I'm doin'?" Goombaw snapped back. "Wedged in between these two sweaty younguns! I'm boilin' in my own juice! This camping trip is the stupidest dang fool idear you ever come up with, Herbert! We'll probably all get et by bears. Tell me, what about bears, Herbert?"

Yeah, I thought. What about bears?

"Ha ha ha ha," Mr. Muldoon laughed. "You don't have to worry about bears. They're more afraid of humans than we are of them."

Well, I thought, that's certainly not true of all humans, particularly one that I know personally. It's probably not true of all bears either. But I kept these thoughts to myself, since Goombaw was doing a thorough job of grilling Mr. Muldoon on the subject. I could tell that the talk of bears was making Mrs. Muldoon nervous, not that she was the only one.

"Let's change the subject, Goombaw," she said.

"Oh, all right. How about mountain lions, Herbert?"

For the rest of the long, hot, dusty ride up to the huckleberry patches, Goombaw harangued Mr. Muldoon about every possible threat to our well-being, from bears to crazed woodcutters. By the time we reached our campsite, she had everyone in such a nervous state that we were almost afraid to get out of the car. Mr. Muldoon stepped out, swiveled his head about as though expecting an attack from any quarter, and then ordered us to help set up camp.

No level area for our tent was immediately apparent, but Crazy Eddie and I finally located one. It was down a steep bank and on the far side of a little creek. Mr. Muldoon, Eddie, and I dragged the bundle of camp gear down the bank and across a log to the little clearing in the brush and trees. In no time at all Mr. Muldoon had constructed a fine shelter out of the tarp. Eddie and I built a fire ring of rocks, and Mrs. Muldoon and Goombaw got a fire going and put coffee on to boil, apparently forgetting that the doctor had told Mr. Muldoon to cut down on his coffee drinking because of his nerves. Eddie and I sampled the fishing in the creek. All in all, the camping trip showed signs of becoming a pleasant experience. Then it got dark.

"I say keep a fire goin' all night," Goombaw advised. "It might help keep the bears off of us."

"There ain't no bears," Mr. Muldoon said. "Now stop worrying about bears. Ha! Bears are more afraid of us than we are of them. Now, everybody get a good night's sleep. We got a lot of huckleberries to pick tomorrow." He stripped down to his long underwear and burrowed into the pile of quilts and blankets Mrs. Muldoon had arranged on the ground.

I pulled my threadbare blanket out of the gunnysack and spread it out in the dirt next to Goombaw.

"Good heavens, Patrick!" Mrs. Muldoon said. "Is that all you have to sleep in, that one little blanket? The nights can get pretty chilly up here in the mountains."

"Oh, I've got more blankets in my sack," I lied. "If it turns cold, I'll just put some more on. But I sleep warm."

As the night dragged on into its full depth, I lay there shivering in my blanket, studying with considerable interest the looming dark shapes the full moon revealed around our camp. Finally, Goombaw and the Muldoons ceased their thrashing about on the hard ground and began to emit the sounds of sleep. I jerked the fur coat out of the gunnysack and buttoned myself into its comforting warmth. I set a mental alarm to awaken me before the Muldoons, so I could conceal the coat before they caught sight of the hideous thing. Then I drifted off into fitful sleep.

"Wazzat?" Goombaw shouted in my ear.

Later, she claimed only to be having a nightmare, but, fortunately for us, she sounded the alarm just in time. In the silence that followed Goombaw's shout, you could almost hear four pairs of eyelids popping open in the dark.

"A bear!" Goombaw shouted. "A bear's got me!"

Since I was lying right next to Goombaw, this announcement aroused my curiosity to no end. I tried to leap to my feet but, wrapped in the fur coat, could only manage to make it to all fours.

"Bear!" screamed Crazy Eddie. "Bear's got Gooooo—!"

"Bear!" shrieked Mrs. Muldoon. "There it is!"

Goombaw made a horrible sound. I could make out the big round whites of her eyes fixed on me in the darkness, no doubt pleading wordlessly with me for help, but what could a small boy do against a bear?

"Holy bleep!" roared Mr. Muldoon. He lunged to his feet, knocking over the ridgepole and dropping the tarp on us and the bear. Figuring Goombaw already for a goner and myself next on the bear's menu, I tore out from under the tarp just in time to see Mr. Muldoon trying to unstick an ax from the stump in which he had embedded it the night before. Even in the shadowy dimness of moonlight, I could see the look of surprise and horror wash over Mr. Muldoon's face as I rushed toward him for protection. He emitted a strangled cry and rushed off through the woods on legs so wobbly it looked as if his knees had come unhinged. Under the circumstances, I could only surmise that the bear was close on my heels, and I raced off after Mr. Muldoon, unable to think of anything better to do. With his abrupt departure, Mr. Muldoon had clearly let it be known that now it was every man for himself.

Bounding over a log with the effortless ease that accompanies total panic, I came upon Mr. Muldoon peeling bark and limbs off a small tree. Since he was only four feet up in the tree, I debated whether to wait for him to gain altitude or to find my own tree. Then Mr. Muldoon caught sight of the bear closing fast on us. He sprang out of the tree and took off again, with me so close behind that I could have reached out and grabbed the snapping flap of his long underwear. The thought did occur to me to do so, because I was nearing exhaustion, and Mr. Muldoon could have towed me along with his underwear flap. Upon later reflection, however, I think it is well that I didn't grab the flap, for it probably would have been a source of considerable embarrassment to both of us.

When I could run no more, I dropped to the ground, deciding I might as well let the bear eat me as run me to death. But the bear was gone. Perhaps he had taken a shortcut through the woods, hoping to cut me and Mr. Muldoon off at a pass. In any case, I never did get to see the bear, narrow as my escape had been. Sweltering in the fur coat, I took the thing off and stuffed it down a hollow stump, glad to be rid of the thing.

When I got back to camp, everyone was gone. I climbed up to the car, inside of which I found Eddie, his mother, and Goombaw, each more or less in one piece.

"Thank heavens," cried Mrs. Muldoon. "We thought the bear had got you! Have you seen Mr. Muldoon?"

I said yes I had, not mentioning that I had seen even more of him than I cared to. Half an hour later, Mr. Muldoon scrambled up the bank to the car. Upon learning that everyone was intact, he explained how he had led the bear away from camp, at considerable risk to himself. I was surprised that he neglected to mention my role in leading the bear off, but didn't think it my place to mention it.

"You got to keep a cool head during a bear attack," Mr. Muldoon explained. "Panic and you're done for."

"Whewee!" Goombaw said. "I smell skunk! Somebody step on a skunk in the dark?"

Then it started to rain. Hard.

Commentary

This story arose out of a segment in another story in which my use of my grandmother's old fur coat as a sleeping bag causes a certain amount of excitement in the other members of my family. I now thought about transporting that coat out into the mountains on a huckleberry-picking expedition with the Muldoon family.

One of my many theories about humor is that it is much funnier for disaster to befall the fellow who is already down and out as opposed to the one who is on top of the world. In other words, it is much funnier for a lowly tramp (Charlie Chaplin) to slip on a banana peel than it is for, say, the town banker. That is why the first two paragraphs of this story are devoted to showing that Mr. Muldoon is already at the end of his rope, one disaster after another befalling him. Now he is hauling his family and young Pat up into the mountains toward yet another disaster.

Many of my stories lead up to a disaster. I first visualize the kind of disaster I want to produce. Then I set about solving the problems that will lead to that disaster.

Problem 1: How will I get the Muldoons and Pat with his fur coat up into the mountains where the bears are? Solution: The Muldoons decide to pick huckleberries and sell them for much needed cash.

Problem 2: Why does Pat keep the coat secret from the Muldoons? Solution: Because he is afraid Mr. Muldoon will tease him about using the coat for a sleeping bag.

Problem 3: How can I put the Muldoons in the proper emotional state so that they will mistake Pat in the coat for a bear? Solution: I bring in Goombaw to instill in the Muldoons her own irrational fear of wild animals.

Problem 4: Why does Pat chase Mr. Muldoon? Solution: Because he thinks Mr. Muldoon can save him from the bear.

And so on. Most stories, at least those that I write, involve solving a set of problems. The tricky part is to make each solution seem natural, reasonable, and most of all, believable.

In this version of the story, Pat doesn't grab the flap of Mr. Muldoon's long underwear. I'm sorry now that I didn't make him grab it. In the stage version of "Goombaw," Pat does grab the flap. It makes for a much more satisfying climax.

"The Night the Bear Ate Goombaw" is collected in a book by the same name. My wife and I were staying in a hotel in Boston while on a promotion tour for the book, several copies of which were scattered around in the back seat of our car. As the Italian doorman was helping us load the car, he noticed the book.

"Did you write that book?" he asked.

"Yes," I said.

"Well, I noticed it in the window of a bookstore the other day, and I said to myself, I wonder what that's about—the Goombaw part."

"Oh, 'Goombaw' is just a name I made up," I explained.

"You don't know what 'Goombaw' means in Italian? he said, clearly astonished. Why, it means a friend who is better than a best friend, almost like your brother, but not quite!"

The doorman was quite astonished to learn that, in my book, a "Goombaw" was a scrawny little old lady.

Once in a while a writer gets lucky, and this is just such a case. For
some reason, all the right elements seemed to converge in the writing of this story.

"Muldoon in Love"

Afterwards, I felt bad for a while about Miss Deets, but Mom told
me to stop fretting about it. She said the problem was, Miss Deets
had just been too delicate to teach third grade in our part of the
country.

Besides being delicate, Miss Deets must also have been rich. I
don't recall ever seeing her wear the same dress two days in a row.
To mention the other extreme, Mr. Craw, one of the seventh-grade
teachers at Delmore Blight Grade School, wore the same suit every
day for thirty years. Once, when Mr. Craw was sick, the suit came to
school by itself and taught his classes, but only Skip Moseby noticed that Mr. Craw wasn't inside the suit. Skip said the suit did a
fair job of explaining dangling participles, which turned out to be a
kind of South American lizard. I would have liked to hear the suit's
lecture, because at the time I was particularly interested in lizards.
But I digress from Miss Deets.

No one could understand why a rich, genteel lady like Miss
Deets would want to teach third grade at Delmore Blight, but on
the first day of school, there she was, smelling of perfume and money,
her auburn hair piled on top of her head, her spectacles hanging by

a cord around her long, slender, delicate neck. We stood there gawking at her, scarcely believing our good fortune in getting this beautiful lady as our very own third-grade teacher.

We boys all fell instantly in love with Miss Deets, but none more than my best friend, Crazy Eddie Muldoon. I loved her quite a bit myself at first, but Eddie would volunteer to skip recess so he could clean the blackboard erasers, whether they needed cleaning or not. For the first month of school, the third grade must have had the cleanest blackboard erasers in the entire history of Delmore Blight Grade School. For me, love was one thing, recess another. God had not intended the two to interfere with each other. But Crazy Eddie now skipped almost every recess in order to help Miss Deets with little chores around the classroom. She was depriving me of my best friend's company, and bit by bit I began to hate her. I wished Miss Deets would go away and never come back. Worse yet, in his continuing efforts to prove his love for Miss Deets, Eddie started studying. He soon became the champion of our weekly spelling bees. "Wonderful, Edward!" Miss Deets would exclaim, when Eddie correctly spelled some stupid word nobody in the entire class would ever have reason to use. Then she would pin a ridiculous little paper star on the front of his shirt, the reward for being the last person standing in the spelling bee. It disgusted me to think Eddie would do all that work, learning how to spell all those words, for nothing more than to have Miss Deets pin a ridiculous little paper star on his shirt.

Then one day Miss Deets made her fateful error. "Now, pupils," she announced, "I think it important for all young ladies and gentlemen to be able to speak in front of groups. So for the next few weeks we are going to have Show and Tell. Each day, one of you will bring one of your more interesting possessions to school, show it to the class, and then tell us all about it. Doesn't that sound like fun?"

Three-fourths of the class, including myself, cringed in horror. We didn't own *any* possessions, let alone interesting ones. Miss Deets looked at me and smiled. "Patrick, would you like to be first?"

I put on my thoughtful expression, as though mentally sorting through all my fascinating possessions to select just the one with which to enthrall the class. My insides, though, churned in terror and embarrassment. What could I possibly bring to Show and Tell? The only thing that came to mind was the family posthole digger. I imagined myself standing up in front of the class and saying, "This is my posthole digger. I dig postholes with it." No, Miss Deets probably had a longer speech in mind. I glanced around the room. Several hands of the rich kids from town were waving frantically for attention.

"Uh, I need more time," I told Miss Deets. Like about fifteen years, I thought, but I didn't tell her that.

"All right, then Lester," Miss Deets said to one of the rich kids. "You may be first."

The next day Lester brought his stamp collection to Show and Tell, and held forth on it for about an hour. An enterprising person could have cut the tedium into blocks and sold it for ice. But Miss Deets didn't seem to notice. "That's wonderful, Lester!" she cried. "Oh, I do think stamp collecting is such a rewarding hobby! Thank you very much, Lester, for such a fine and educational presentation. Would you like to clean the blackboard erasers during recess?"

I glanced at Crazy Eddie. He was yawning. Eddie had a habit of yawning to conceal his occasional moments of maniacal rage. Good, I thought.

At recess, Eddie refused to play. He stood with his hands jammed in his pockets, watching Lester on the third-grade fire escape, smugly pounding the blackboard erasers together. "Did you ever see anything more boring than that stupid stamp collection of Lester's?" he said to me.

"I think I did once," I said. "But it was so boring I forgot what it was."

"I've got to come up with something for Show and Tell, something really good," Eddie said. "What do you think about a posthole digger?"

Lester's stamp collection, however, was merely the beginning of a competition that was to escalate daily as each succeeding rich kid tried to top the one before. There were coin collections, doll collections, baseball-card collections, model airplanes powered by their own little engines, electric trains that could chew your heart out just looking at them, and on and on until we had exhausted the supply of rich kids in class. We were now down to us country kids, among whom there were no volunteers for Show and Tell. Miss Deets thought we were merely shy. She didn't realize we had nothing to show and tell about.

Rudy Griddle, ordered by Miss Deets to be the first of us to make a presentation, shuffled to the front of the class, his violent shaking surrounding him with a mist of cold sweat. He opened a battered cigar box and tilted it up so we could see the contents. "This here's my collection of cigarette butts," he said. "I pick 'em up along the road. You'll notice there ain't any shorter than an inch. If they's an inch or longer they's keepers. I just collect them for educational purposes. Thank you." He returned to his desk and sat down.

The class turned to look at Miss Deets. Her mouth was twisted in revulsion. Suddenly, someone started clapping! Crazy Eddie Muldoon was applauding! And somebody else called out, "Yay, good job, Rudy!" The rest of us country kids joined in the applause and cheering and gave Rudy a standing ovation. He deserved it. After all, he had shown us the way. From now on, Show and Tell would *really* be interesting.

Farley Karp brought in the skunk hide he had tanned himself and gave a very interesting talk on the process, even admitting that he had made a few mistakes, but after all, it was the first skunk hide he had ever tanned. He said he figured from what he had learned on the first one, the next skunk hide he tanned he probably could cut the smell by a good fifty percent, which would be considerable.

Bill Stanton brought in his collection of dried wildlife droppings, which he had glued to a pine board in a tasteful display and varnished. It was a fine collection, with each item labeled as to its source.

Manny Fogg, who had been unable to think of a single thing to bring to Show and Tell, was fortunate enough to cut his foot with a double-bitted ax three days before his presentation and was able to come in and unwrap the bandages and show us the wound, which his mother had sewed shut with gut leader. It was totally ghastly but also very interesting, and educational too, particularly if you chopped firewood with a double-bitted ax, as most of us did.

Show and Tell had begun to tell on Miss Deets. Her face took on a wan and haunted look, and she became cross and jumpy. Once I think she went to the cloakroom and cried, because when she returned, her eyes were all red and glassy. That was the time Laura Ann Struddel brought in the chicken that all the other Struddel chickens had pecked half the feathers off of. Laura Ann had set the chicken on Miss Deets's desk and was using a pointer to explain the phenomenon. The chicken, looking pleased to be on leave from the other chickens, but also a little excited at being the subject of Show and Tell, committed a small indiscretion right there on Miss Deets's desk.

"Oh, my gahhh . . ." Miss Deets gasped, her face going as red as dewberry wine, while we third-graders had a good laugh. This, after all, was the first humor introduced into Show and Tell. From then on, those of us who still had to do Show and Tell tried to work a little comedy into our presentations, but nobody topped the chicken.

So many great things had been brought to Show and Tell by the other country kids that I had become desperate to find something of equal interest. Finally, I went with my road-killed toad, explaining how it had been flattened by a truck and afterwards had dried on the pavement, until I came along and peeled it up to save for posterity. The toad went over fairly well, and I even got a couple of laughs out of it, which is about all you can expect from a toad. Even so, Miss Deets chose not to compliment me on my performance. She just sat there slumped in her chair, fanning herself with a sheaf of arithmetic papers. I thought she looked a tad green, but that could have been my imagination.

Now only Margaret Fisher and Crazy Eddie were left to do their Show and Tells. I knew Eddie was planning to use several pig organs from a recent butchering, provided they hadn't spoiled too much by the time he got to use them. But Margaret changed his plans.

She brought in a cardboard box and proudly carried it to the front of the room. Miss Deets backed off to a far corner, her hands fluttering nervously about her mouth, as Margaret pried up the lid of the box. A mother cat and four cute baby kittens stuck out their heads. Everyone *ooh*ed and *aah*ed. Miss Deets went over and picked up one of the kittens and told Margaret what a wonderful idea she'd had, to bring in the kittens, and would Margaret like to clean the blackboard erasers at recess?

At recess, Eddie was frantic. "I can't use the pig stuff now," he said. "I got to come up with something live that has cute babies."

"How about using Henry?" I suggested.

"Yeah, Henry's cute, all right, but he don't have no babies."

"Hey, I've got an idea! I said. "I know some things we can use and just *say* they're his babies. But you'd better call Henry a girl's name. Heck, Miss Deets won't know the difference."

Eddie smiled. I knew he was thinking he would soon have back his old job of cleaning the blackboard erasers for Miss Deets.

Everyone in third grade counted on Crazy Eddie Muldoon to come up with a spectacular grand finale for Show and Tell. An air of great expectation filled the room as Eddie, carrying a large pail, marched up to make his presentation. Even Miss Deets seemed to be looking forward to the event, possibly because it was the last of Show and Tell, but no doubt also because she expected one of her favorite pupils to come up with something memorable.

With the flair of the natural showman, Eddie deftly flipped off the lid of the lard pail in which he had punched air holes.

"And now, ladies and gentlemen," he announced, "here is Henrietta Muldoon . . . my pet garter snake." He held up the writhing Henry.

Miss Deets sucked in her breath with such force she shuffled papers on desks clear across the room.

"And that's not all," Crazy Eddie continued, although it was plain from the look on Miss Deets's face that Henry all by himself was excessive. Beaming, Eddie thrust his other hand into the pail.

"Here, ladies and gentlemen, are her babies!"

He held up the squirming mass of nightcrawlers he had collected the evening before.

At first I thought the sound was the distant wail of a fire siren, a defective one, with a somewhat higher pitch than normal. It rose slowly and steadily in volume, quavering, piercing, until it vibrated the glass in the windows and set every hair of every third-grader straining at its follicle. We were stunned to learn that human vocal cords could produce such an unearthly sound, and those of a third-grade teacher at that.

Mr. Cobb, the principal, came and led Miss Deets away, and we never saw her again. We heard later that she had gone back to teach school in the city, where all the kids were rich and she could lead a peaceful and productive life.

As the door closed behind her, I turned to Eddie and said, "I think you've cleaned your last blackboard eraser for Miss Deets."

"Yeah, I suspect you're right," he said sadly. Then he brightened. "But you got to admit, that was one whale of a Show and Tell!"

Commentary

"Muldoon in Love" is probably my favorite of all the hundreds of stories and articles I've written over the years. If I like this story so much, why don't I write stories just like it all the time? Because I can't, that's why. Sometimes all the right elements for a story come together as if by magic, and that is what happened here. I didn't make this story. It simply happened. So one keeps on writing and writing and writing, always with the hope the magic will come again. And sometimes it does.

The opening raises a question that will be answered only at the end of the story: What happened to Miss Deets? That gives the story a tension that should pull the reader all the way to the end, out of curiosity if nothing else. Whether writing a story or an article, or a novel for that matter, it is always a good idea to raise a question that will be answered at the end of the work. And don't ever raise a question you don't answer. Otherwise, your readers will hate you for life. Remember the novel by the graduate creative writing student in which one of his characters disappears and is never mentioned again? I thought the novel was monumentally boring and would never have given it a second thought, except I couldn't get out of my mind the sudden disappearance of the character. I finally hunted down the student and demanded, "What happened to Duke?" He said he made Duke disappear without explanation because he thought that would add some interest to the story. Well, it certainly did. And lord knows, it needed some. WRITING RULE 4057: NEVER RAISE QUESTIONS YOU DON'T ANSWER.

The viewpoint of "Love" is fairly complex, because it is obvious that the story is being told by the adult Pat about something that occurred during his youth, but the viewpoint throughout is actually that of the eight-year-old Pat. Everything that happens is seen and experienced through the eyes, the emotions, the innocence and the ignorance of a boy in third grade. This is a different kind of viewpoint than in, say, *The Adventures of Huckleberry Finn*, where we also experience the story through the innocence and ignorance of a young boy. But there the young Huck himself narrates the story. In "Love," the storyteller looks back and through the distorting prism of himself as a young boy, and it is that distorting prism that makes the story work. The adult narrator, for example, would never view Miss Deets as rich on the basis that she never wore the same dress two days in a row. Had the adult Pat, the narrator, retained the viewpoint, he would have had to write something like, "I actually thought Miss Deets was rich because she never wore the same dress two days in a row." Doesn't work. So why not let the eight-year-old Pat narrate the story? Because he lived in a different and distant time, and the young Pat would have to narrate the story as if it were in the near present, when the world of even the rural child is much different than it was a half century ago. WRITING RULE 405: DON'T CONFUSE THE READER WITH TIME SHIFTS. There is also an element of nostalgia here that would be lost if the story were told in present time.

What about the Recognition Factor? Well, everyone was a child once, and thought as a child, felt as a child and acted as a child. That is the major Recognition Factor. Surely everyone found himself or herself in some kind of predicament at school and can easily recall as an adult the feelings of desperation that predicament produced. The Recognition Factor doesn't deal in specifics, like posthole digger and cannibalized chickens, but in generalities, like desperation and triumph.

Conflict is essential to any story, and here a number of conflicts occur between Pat and Eddie, between the teacher and the poor kids, between the poor kids and the "rich" kids, and the central conflict, between poverty and Show and Tell, the obstacle to be overcome.

This story is fiction. It never happened. So where did it come from? Its initial conception arose from a gritty, firsthand experience of my being a poor rural kid in school. That experience is what I hoped to capture and turn into a story of some kind. I wrote the first paragraph without knowing where the story was going, except I realized Miss Deets had a problem of some kind. Then the "voice" of that first paragraph seemed to take over the story and carry it along about as fast as I could invent the various situations. To me, the voice and viewpoint are essentially the story.

Newton: "Mean Tents" is one of your convergence stories, isn't it, Pat?

Very perceptive, Newt. The actual convergence doesn't occur until Pat and Eddie create their "mean tent" out of gunny sacks. From that point on, all elements of the story converge on a particular point in time and a particular point in space.

"Mean Tents"

I once shot three arrows through my cousin Buck's brand-new wall tent. This may not seem remarkable to you, but it was to Buck. I can still recall several of his remarks, in fact, even though at the time they were made I was vaulting a high board fence as he tried to tear off one of my legs. It happened like this.

I was out in Buck's backyard, practicing with his bow and arrows, when he showed up carrying a large bundle of canvas on his shoulder. Buck was four years older than I, or about twenty. He had a job and could afford to buy all kinds of neat hunting and fishing stuff. I could use his stuff anytime I wanted, provided Buck wasn't around. His mother, my Aunt Sophie, who thought highly of me, was always eager to help the less fortunate, who in this case happened to be me. She would unlock the door to Buck's bedroom and even help me disarm some of the booby traps her ingenious son had set to maim or kill me, should I sneak in to use his stuff.

"What are you doing with my bow?" Buck snarled, even though it was perfectly obvious I was target-practicing.

Pretending not to hear, I said, "Gosh, Buck, what's that you got there?"

Instantly his mood flip-flopped. "A new wall tent!" he exclaimed. "I just bought it. Wait till you see this baby. I'm gonna take it up into the mountains next fall and set up a hunting camp like you wouldn't believe. I got this little woodstove I'm gonna put in it for heat, and a little table and chairs, and a couple of cots . . ."

Having distracted him from uncharitable thoughts about my use of his bow, I helped him drag the tent across the backyard to a flat area about ten feet from the bale of hay I had been using as a target. We soon had the tent pitched, its canvas taut and gleaming in the sun. I had to admit it was a nice-looking tent. Buck thought it was beautiful. We stepped back to admire it.

While he was in such a good mood, I said, "Yeah, that's a terrific tent, Buck. Mind if I shoot a few more arrows?"

"What? Oh, yeah, go ahead. Now, you see that canvas? It's special canvas. That canvas is windproof and . . ."

I casually let fly with an arrow at the target. The arrow curved like a boomerang in flight, and with a tiny *phutt!*, zipped through the roof of the tent.

". . . waterproof." Buck's eyes widened. His jaw gaped slowly, as if held by a weak spring.

"It was an accident, Buck," I cried, snatching up another arrow. "Your arrow must have been crooked. See, I shot it just like this."

Phutt! The second arrow zipped through the tent!

I could not believe this was happening. It was as if the tent had a magnetic attraction for arrows. I glanced at Buck. He seemed okay, except for possible paralysis of his entire nervous system. His lips made little jerking motions, but otherwise he was immobile.

"I can explain, Buck. Some of these arrows are crooked. They curve when you shoot them. Now this arrow is straight. Watch, it'll hit the target. Those other two arrows were crooked. It's not my fault you have crooked arrows. Here goes."

"*Phutt!*"

It was the strangest occurrence I had ever encountered. Having considerable interest in science, I would have liked to study how not one, not two, but three arrows could be drawn ten feet off course and through the roof of a tent. By this time, however, Buck had come unthawed and unwrapped, cutting short any hope I might have had for discovering the attraction of tent canvas for arrows. I took my usual escape route over the back fence, sacrificing only half a pantleg to the clawing hands of my crazed cousin.

Thirty years later Buck would still be convinced that I had deliberately shot the arrows through the tent for no better reason than to aggravate him. But I was innocent. The guilty party was the tent itself, its motive nothing more than to cause me trouble. In fact, tents have always had it in for me.

Remember the old Interior-Frame Umbrella Tent? The one with the contraption called the "spider" that was supposed to hold everything together? We used one of those tents for fifteen years. Every camping family in America owned one. Few people know, however, that they were originally developed by research psychologists as a stress test to determine the limits of sanity. Later, the U.S. Army got hold of the I-FUT, as the Interior-Frame Umbrella Tent was known, and experimented with it as a means of training recruits in hand-to-hand combat. When it was rejected by the army as too demoralizing to the troops, tent manufacturers decided the I-FUT was perfect for campers. After all, they reasoned, campers go out seeking hardship and adventure. Pitching the I-FUT would provide the average camper with about all the hardship and adventure he could stand.

Even though we last used our I-FUT more than ten years ago, before we moved up to the Exterior-Frame Tent, I can still recall vividly the typical routine of pitching it:

I have just staked down the floor of the tent. Tent came with tough plastic stakes, which greatly eased this task, but of course all of the stakes have now been lost. I have substituted crooked pieces of tree branch for the plastic stakes, pounding them in with a flat rock. This results in my having to perform the Crouch Hop, a primitive dance, in which the performer holds one hand between his thighs and hops about chanting "Hai-yi-yi-yi!" and other chants, while his wife holds her hands over the ears of the youngest child.

Now comes the dreaded part. I must crawl into the shapeless mass of canvas to insert the interior frame. Powdery remains of last year's insects come sprinkling down onto my face. The tiny, stickery legs are the worst, particularly when they go down the back of your shirt collar. I sneeze. As a cause of sneezing, powdered bug is just as bad as pepper. Some people think it's a whole lot worse. Squeamish people almost always abandon camping during this phase of pitching the I-FUT.

Not all the bugs are dead. At least one daddy longlegs will have survived the winter for the sole purpose of racing up under your pantleg. When you are standing in the dark with a collapsed tent around your head, a daddy longlegs racing for your vitals feels as big as a Dungeness crab.

The part of the frame called the "spider" has four arms, each of which extends out to a corner of the tent roof. The upright poles, in theory at least, insert into the outer ends of the spider arms. A short, sharp-edged pipe protrudes downward from the center of the spider. The sharp end of this pipe is placed on top of your head to hold the spider in place while you attach the poles. This explains why all old-time tent campers have a series of little overlapping circles on the tops of their heads.

I am now standing in the tent with one spider charging up my leg and the other "spider" cutting doughnut holes in my scalp. Quickly I insert the first pole into the spider, but it won't stay in place by itself until another pole has taken the slack out of the tent. I balance on one leg and hold the pole up with the other.

"Quick," I yell to my little helpers outside. "Hand Daddy another pole." I immediately hear the sound of scurrying feet, followed by heated argument.

"I got it first! Leggo!"

"Aaaaaah!," I say. "Hur-reeeee! Aaaaa!"

"Gimme that pole!"

"Aaakkkk!" I say.

"I got it! Here I come, Daddy!"

I can hear little feet charging for the door of the tent. "Easy! Easy!!" I yell, but too late. The pole comes through the flap of the tent like a spear thrust.

"Just think," my wife says later, "if we had just one more kid, you could stand one in each corner of the tent to hold a pole while you hook up the spider."

"That possibility has just been rendered academic," I say. "So maybe we'll buy a camper."

I still have our old I-FUT out in the corner of the garage, and it's in surprisingly good shape. My wife says I should donate it to the Salvation Army so it can be passed on to a needy family. I point out to her that needy families already have enough problems without my inflicting an I-FUT on them. Besides, I like to keep the I-FUT around for old time's sake. Whenever I get depressed, I can go out and kick it hard several times. Immediately I feel better.

My very first tent was a teepee. I made it out of three crooked branches and a blanket when I was about six years old. It served me well for an hour or two, until I decided to take the chill out of the air by building a fire in it. Presently my father came wandering out of the house and saw me standing by my teepee, which was putting up little puffs of smoke. It is a traumatic experience, let me tell you, for a small child to see his father stomp out his teepee! To complicate matters, Dad never understood what it was he had stomped out. He thought I just liked to set fire to blankets.

Speaking of strained relations between father and son, I'm reminded of the time a couple of years later that Crazy Eddie Muldoon and I made a tent out of gunnysacks. We had found the sacks in the back of the Muldoon barn. Although they were moldy and half rotten and flecked with dried cow manure, Eddie said they would still make a good tent. We obtained a large pair of shears and a curved sacking needle from his father's toolbox, which Mr. Muldoon had thoughtfully left within our reach. By suppertime the tent was finished.

I tried to conceal my disappointment over the appearance of the finished product. To me it looked more like a large, shaggy cocoon than a tent. Crazy Eddie, however, was delighted with it, as he was with all his creations.

"We'll set it up in the backyard and sleep in it tonight," he announced.

"Okay," I said. Eddie and I had been trying to sleep out all night in his backyard for most of the summer, but our efforts had always been thwarted by the elements—torrential darkness being the most frequent. So far, our best time had been 9:30. But Eddie had recently discovered a secret weapon: his father's powerful, six-battery flashlight. Furthermore, his father was away on a trip and wasn't expected back until late that night. We would simply leave the flashlight on all night and return it to his father's shop in the morning before he was awake and hovering about, eyeing us with suspicion. Mr. Muldoon would never know the difference. It would teach him a good lesson, too, for guffawing and teasing us about our failures at sleeping out past 9:30, even though we gave him detailed reports on the large, weird creatures we had seen prowling the yard.

The disaster resulting from this innocent plan cannot be properly understood without knowing the exact sequence of events, which is a follows:

7:30 pm: Crazy Eddie and I haul a quilt, a blanket, and two pillows out to our tent and make our bed.

8:00 pm: We crawl under the quilt and lie there looking at the stars through the roof of our tent. We have routinely checked the laces on our tennis shoes for tightness. Kids we know have thrown a shoe coming out of the starting blocks on their way into the house on a dark night. The loss of traction on one side has caused them to waste precious seconds running in a circle.

9:00 pm: The condition known as "pitch dark" has been achieved. Crazy Eddie flips on the powerful flashlight. The beam shoots out through our tent and illuminates the countryside for a hundred yards. It seems adequate. Eddie and I exchange smiles of confidence.

10:00 pm: Mrs. Muldoon turns off the house lights and goes to bed. Only the feeble porch light remains on. A sense of apprehension fills the gunnysack tent. The beam of the flashlight has weakened.

10:15 pm: Mr. Muldoon gets in his car and begins the long drive home. He turns on the radio to listen to country-western music.

11:00 pm: The power of the flashlight has diminished to that of a firefly. The porch light provides some illumination. A dark shadow passes over the tent. Eddie and I dig starting blocks with the heels of our tennis shoes through the floor of the tent.

11:05 pm: Mr. Muldoon flicks the radio dial to "The Creaking Door." Tonight's program is about a mummy that tracks down and takes revenge on an archaeologist for disturbing its tomb. Mr.

Muldoon shudders at the dry, rustling sound of the mummy's loose wrapping as they drag across the floor. The mummy says, "Urrr-uh! Urrr-uh!" which may not be all that articulate, but is pretty good for a mummy.

11:25 *pm*: Mr. Muldoon pulls into his driveway. On the radio, the archaeologist is screaming, "No! No! Stay away from meeee!" Then there's the sound of wrappings scrapping across the floor. "Urrr-uh," says the mummy. "Urrr-uh!" Mr. Muldoon shuts off the radio, gets out of the car and heads for the house. Then he goes back and shuts off the car lights. The wind rustles in the bushes. Mr. Muldoon rushes into the house and turns on the lights.

Eddie and I have heard Mr. Muldoon drive in. Our flashlight is dead. Our tennis shoes are dug into the starting blocks, but now we must wait for Mr. Muldoon to go to bed. Otherwise he will tease us unmercifully. Outside, there is a strange rustling sound, coming closer and closer. It's a good thing we haven't heard the mummy program.

11:35 *pm*: Mr. Muldoon shuts off the kitchen light *and* the porch light. He has no reason to expect his son and me to be outside in the dark. He goes into the bathroom to take a shower, still thinking about the mummy.

11:45 *pm*: The rustling around the tent has increased. Eddie is fumbling with the knots on the door, but can't untie them in the dark. In a few minutes, Mr. Muldoon will be in bed asleep.

11:46 *pm*: Eddie's dog, Oscar, returns from a date at a neighboring farm and slumps down exhausted on the porch. Oscar has no reason to expect Eddie and me to be outside in the dark.

11:50 *pm*: Mr. Muldoon thinks he detects a sore throat coming on. He walks into the darkened kitchen, pours some salt into a glass of hot water and begins to gargle. He is wearing only a towel, wrapped around his middle.

11:50:30 *pm*: Eddie groans, "I can't get these dang knots untied in the dark. Let's go inside. We can take the tent off in there." A shadow passes over the tent, accompanied by a rustling sound to our rear. We shove our feet through the burlap floor and, hugging the tent around us, hit the starting blocks.

11:50:31 *pm*: On the porch, Oscar opens his bleary eyes. A large, amorphous shape is charging him! Almost on top of him! Probably going to eat him! He tries to bark but has momentarily swallowed his tongue. "Urrr-uh!" he growls. "Urrr-uh!"

11:50:32 *pm*: Eddie and I crash through the door into the kitchen. Instantly we hear a horrible sound. We don't know what it is, never before having heard a naked man surprised in mid-gargle by a gunnysack tent. Oscar follows us into the house still trying to bark. "URRR-UH! URRR-UH!" Water splashes on the floor and there is the sound of naked feet frantically trying to get traction on slippery linoleum.

"*Gargle, gurgle, choke*! cries Mr. Muldoon. "St-stay—*hack, gargle—away—choke*—from meeeeee!"

We didn't get the mess all sorted out and reconstructed until the next morning. Mr. Muldoon seemed quite embarrassed by the whole episode and never again teased us for abandoning a backyard camp in the middle of the night. Later though, he enjoyed recalling the episode of the gunnysack tent and having a good laugh over it. I was away at college by then, however, and never got to hear him.

Commentary

Once again this story is shaped by the editorial demand that I write to a certain length, 2,500 to 3,000 words. My shooting the arrows through Cousin Buck's new tent—an actual occurrence—and the I-FUT may be thought of as fillers. My main purpose was to write about the gunnysack tent, but it by itself would not reach the required length, unless I padded it out. Humor demands concision in writing; consequently, you are always trying to achieve a particular effect in the fewest possible words, always a good rule for writing in general but particularly so for humor. So if you must pad out a piece to reach a certain length, do it by adding anecdotes, not merely by adding words.

Obviously, shooting arrows through someone's new tent is not funny, particularly to the person who owns the tent. To develop humor out of this situation I had to create an adversarial relationship between Buck and me, and provide the reader with at least a suggestion of our contrasting personalities. The humor results from extending the normal tension between us to an extreme level. This tension is further fueled by misunderstanding. Buck simply can't believe that Pat's shooting an arrow through his tent could have been anything but maliciously deliberate, an impression reinforced by Pat's shooting two more arrows through the tent in an effort to prove his innocence.

Because "Mean Tents" was originally written for *Field & Stream*, I knew that my audience would be familiar with the interior-frame umbrella tent. The Recognition Factor would kick in, because anyone owning one of these tents would have had as much trouble erecting it as I did. The Recognition Factor might also be thought of as the "Ain't That The Truth!" factor. Probably no one could understand my description of the "spider" and the difficulties of using it, unless he had actually owned an I-FUT. Umbrella tents and their "spiders" being rare these days, anyone writing humorously about them could not count on most of his readers having shared a similar experience, and that would be a big handicap to overcome. Typically, the reader will find the familiar experience funnier than the unique one.

The gunnysack tent is the real story here. I have used it in my stage show, "A Fine and Pleasant Misery" with very satisfying results. It is a fairly complex piece, one I like to think of as a convergence story. We have all the parts converging on a single point in space and time, the Muldoon kitchen at approximately midnight.

Again it was important to establish a relationship early in the story, this time between Mr. Muldoon and the boys. Mr. Muldoon's teasing the boys about their fear of the dark sets up his own horrified response to the gunnysack tent. There also is some kind of continuing conflict between the boys and Eddie's pa. Mr. Muldoon regards them with suspicion, probably because these two kids are always up to something.

A couple of misunderstandings operate here. Oscar the dog thinks the tent is some horrible beast about to devour him. Mr. Muldoon makes a connection between the gunnysack and the mummy on the radio show he has just been listening to, an impression enhanced by Oscar's repeating the mummy sound, "Urrr-uh."

A naked person is funnier than a clothed one, and so I decided it would be nice to have Mr. Muldoon bare in the kitchen. The thought process went something like this: "I want Mr. Muldoon to be naked in the kitchen when the boys burst through the door. Why would he be naked? Because he just took a shower. But why would he go out to the kitchen? Hmmmm. Oh, because he senses a sore throat coming on and wants to gargle with salt water. The salt is in the kitchen. Perfect!" The gargling also created the horrible sounds to fuel the fear of the already terrified boys: yet another misunderstanding.

The use of specific clock times serves a number of functions. It keeps the reader oriented in time to the sequence of events, without the use of "then," "after that," "next" and so on. Keeping the reader oriented in time is always a problem for a writer and countless words are spent for this purpose alone. The clock times solve this problem and allow for much greater compression of the story. The times give the impression of a ticking down to an explosion of some sort and thusly the building up of anticipation in the reader, or at least that was my hope. The clock times also suggest an increasing momentum in the story, because the intervals between elements in the sequence become progressively more brief, as we sense the various parts converging on each other.

It is interesting to observe a theater audience reacting to this story. The audience responds very much as I imagined it would when I was writing the story for print. It senses the convergence. The mere addition of one little part, the sleepy Oscar flopping down on the porch, for example, produces roars of laughter, even though there is nothing inherently funny about a dog lying down on a porch. The audience knows that dog is there for no good—but what? This kind of anticipation in an audience is one of the more difficult effects to achieve in humor, and I only wish I could pull it off on a regular basis. 🚲

Newton: *If I were a real person, Pat, instead of just another one of your dumb characters, I bet I would have had a bike just like the one in "The Two-Wheeled ATV."*

You're right about that, Newt. I'm sure you would have had just such a bike. There probably is no single implement of youth so universally identified with as the first bicycle. A bike is a perfect Recognition Factor for a humorous story.

"The Two-Wheeled ATV"

My first all-terrain vehicle was a one-wheel drive, and it could take you anywhere you had nerve and guts enough to pedal it.

Most of the other kids around had decent, well-mannered bicycles of distinct makes and models. Mine was a balloon-tired monster born out of wedlock halfway between the junkyard and the secondhand store. Some local fiend had built it with his own three hands and sold it to my mother for about the price of a good milk cow.

For two cents or even a used jawbreaker, I would have beaten it to death with a baseball bat, but I needed it for transportation. And transportation, then as now, was the name of the game.

You could walk to some good fishing holes, all right, but when the guys you were with all rode bikes, you had to walk pretty fast.

Perhaps the worst thing about the Bike, as I called it within hearing range of my mother, was that you simply could not ride it in a manner that allowed you to retain any sense of dignity let alone *savoir-faire.* The chief reason for this was that the seat was permanently adjusted for a person about six-foot-four. I was a person about five-foot-four. The proportions of the handlebars suggested strongly that they had been stolen from a tricycle belonging to a four-year-old midget. The result of this unhappy combination was that wherever I went on the Bike my rear was always about three inches higher than my shoulder blades.

I tried never to go any place on the Bike where girls from school might see me, since it was difficult if not impossible in that position to maintain the image I was cultivating among them of a dashing, carefree playboy.

The seat on the Bike was of the kind usually found on European racing bikes. The principle behind the design of this seat is that the rider goes to beat hell the sooner to get off of it. The idea for heel-and-toe walking races was conceived by someone watching the users of these particular seats footing it back home after a race.

To get the proper effect of one of these seats, you might spend a couple of hours sitting balanced on the end of a baseball bat—the small end. Put a doily on it for cushioning.

Whatever the other guys thought of my appearance on the Bike, they had respect for me. I was the fastest thing around on two wheels, thanks to that seat.

The Bike had a couple of little tricks it did with its chain that the Marquis de Sade would have envied. One was that it would wait until you had just started down a long, steep, curving hill and then reach up with its chain and wind your pant leg into the sprocket. This move was doubly ingenious, since the chain not only prevented you from putting on the coaster brakes, it also shackled you to a hurtling death-machine. Many was the time that a streamlined kid on a bike streaked silently past cars, trucks and motorcycles, on grades where a loose roller skate could break the sound barrier.

The Bike's other favorite trick was to throw the chain off when you needed it most. This usually happened when you were trying to outrun one of the timber wolves the neighbors kept for watchdogs. You would be standing up pedaling for all you were worth, leaving a trail of sweat and burned rubber two inches wide on the road behind you. The wolf would be a black snarl coming up fast to your rear. Then the chain would jump its sprocket and drop you with a crunch on the crossbar, the pedals still spinning furiously under your feet. The wolf gnawed on you until you got the chain back on the sprocket or until he got tired and went home.

The standard method for getting off the Bike was to spring clear and let it crash. If it got the chance, it would grab you by the pant leg at the moment of ejection and drag you along to grim destruction.

The Bike would sometimes go for weeks without the front wheel bouncing off. This was to lure you into a false sense of security. You would be rattling hell-bent for home past the neighbors, and for a split second you would see the front wheel pulling away from you. The fork would hit the ground and whip you over the handlebars. Before you had your breath back, the wolf was standing on your belly reading the menu.

I spent half my waking moments repairing the Bike and the other half repairing myself. Until I was old enough to drive, I went around looking like a commercial for Band-Aids and Mercurochrome. I hated to stop the Bike along the highway long enough to pick up an empty beer bottle for fear people would stop their cars and try to rush me to a doctor. Even on one of its good days, the Bike looked like an accident in which three people had been killed.

Much as I hated the Bike, I have to admit that it was one of the truly great all-terrain vehicles. It could navigate streams, cross fallen logs, smash through brush, follow a mountain trail, and in general do just about anything but climb trees. Several times it did try to climb trees, but the damage to both of us was sufficient to make continued efforts in that direction seem impractical and unrewarding.

Our bicycles in those days were the chief mode of transportation for ninety percent of our camping trips. Occasionally even today I see people use bicycles for camping. They will be zipping along the road on ten-speed touring bikes, their ultra-light camping gear a neat little package on the rear fender. When we went camping on our one-speed bikes, it looked as if we had a baby elephant on the handlebars and the mother on behind.

Loading a bicycle for a camping trip was not simply a remarkable feat of engineering, it was a blatant defiance of all the laws of physics. First of all, there may have been ultra-light camping gear in those days, but we didn't own any of it. Our skillet alone weighed more than one of today's touring bikes, and a bedroll in cold weather, even without the feather bed, was the weight and size of a bale of straw. The tent was a tarp that worked winters as a haystack cover. A good portion of our food was carried in the quart jars our mothers had canned it in. Then there were all the axes, hatchets, saws, machetes and World War II surplus bayonets, without which no camping trip was complete. And of course, I could never leave behind my jungle hammock, the pride of my life, just in case I happened to come across a jungle.

The standard packing procedure was to dump most of your stuff into the center of the tarp, roll the tarp up into a bundle, tie it together with half a mile of rope, and then find nine boys and a man to lift it to the back fender of the Bike. Anything left over was rolled up in the jungle hammock and tied to the diminutive handlebars. The hardware was distributed evenly around the outside of the two massive bundles, just in case you had a sudden need for an ax or a bayonet.

Then you sprang onto the saddle and pedaled with all the fury you could generate from ninety-eight pounds of bone and muscle. The Bike would howl in rage, the twin humps of camp gear would shudder and sway like a sick camel, and slowly, almost imperceptibly, the whole catastrophe would move out of the yard and wobble off down the road on some incredible journey.

Sometimes during the winter now, when the cold awakens in my bones and flesh the ache of a thousand old injuries, I suddenly will recall in vivid detail the last few terrifying moments of the Bike's existence as a recognizable entity.

A ragged gypsy band of us had just begun another trip into the mountains on our camel-humped ATV's. As usual, I was far out in the lead, the hatchet-head bicycle seat urging me on.

There was a hill about three miles from my home called Sand Creek Hill, a name deceptive in its lack of color and description. By rights the hill should have been called Deadman's Drop or Say Goodbye Hill. Loggers drove their trucks down it with one foot on the running board and one hand clutching a rosary—even the atheists.

Just as I crested the hill and started my descent, whom should I notice coming up it, but one of our neighbors' wolves, apparently returning home after a hard night of killing elk in the mountains. From fifty yards away I could see his face brighten when he caught sight of me hurtling toward him like doom on two wheels. He crouched expectantly, his eyes happily agleam.

The chain, not to be outdone, chose that moment to eat my pant leg half way up to the knee. I expected to be abandoned by the front wheel any second. The washboard road rattled my bones; axes, saws, and bayonets filled the air on all sides; and the great straining mass of the rear pack threatened to collapse on me. With one last great effort, I aimed a quick kick at the wolf, ripped the pant leg free and threw myself into space. I bounced four times to distribute the injuries evenly about my body, and finally, using my nose for a brake, slid to a stop.

The Bike apparently self-destructed shortly after my departure. Probably the front wheel came off and the two packs took it from there, ripping and tearing, mashing and grinding until there was nothing left but a streak of assorted rubble stretching off down the hill.

Even the wolf was somewhat shaken by the impact of the crash. He stared at the wreckage in silent awe, almost forgetting my one good leg which he held in his slack jaws.

When I was up and around once more, my mother bought me a car, my second ATV. She got it from a local fiend, who had built it with his own three hands, but that's another story.

Commentary

One day several months after "The Two-Wheeled ATV" was first published in *Field & Stream,* I received a hand-written letter from a woman who said she was a painting restorer at the Metropolitan Museum of Modern Art. The letter went something like this:

"It is pouring rain outside and I am sitting here in an Automat in midtown Manhattan. I looked around for something to read while I finished my cup of coffee and donut, but all I could find was a stupid outdoor magazine. As I listlessly thumbed through it, I came across your article about your first bicycle.

"I thought it was wonderful. I had a bike just like it when I was growing up in Brooklyn."

The lady then went into a lengthy and humorous and some-what bawdy description of her own bicycle. This is the Recognition Factor in action. Here was a person with whom I had absolutely nothing in common, a person who clearly detested outdoor magazines and the outdoors in general. But she connected with the bicycle. Almost every person in the country had a bicycle of some kind when he or she was a child, and no doubt suffered many of the same frustrations with their two-wheeled vehicle as I did with mine. Because so many people could identify with my bicycle troubles as a child, the *Reader's Digest* reprinted this story for its own massive audience. Bicycles are universal.

As with my bike, I sometimes will focus on a single object, turn it this way and that in my mind, and see if it can't be turned into a story. Crazy Eddie Muldoon and I also had Radio Flyer wagons that caused us a good deal of damage. For some reason I've never written about the wagons but probably will do so someday. Other objects I've written about are tennis shoes, a BB gun, a hat, a tent, a fur coat, a hatchet, my first pair of glasses, a ladder, trailer lights, my first knife, and so on. All of these are fairly commonplace objects that almost everyone is familiar with—in other words, the Recognition Factor.

I have always been fascinated—and amused—by the way people eat ice-cream cones. Deciding where to take the first lick, they study the cone as if it were a bomb that would explode if licked in the wrong place. Be my guest: write a humorous story about people eating ice-cream cones. I can't think of anything with a higher Recognition Factor than ice-cream cones.

The boring trivia of everyday life are the grist for the mill of the humor writer. Erma Bombeck would tell you so, too. No one has ever handled the Recognition Factor better than Erma.

Newton: You seem quite often to write about aging. Do you have a hang-up about growing older?

No, Newton, only about *not* growing older. Actually, I am quite interested in the process of aging and how people deal with it, and yes, how I deal with it. Getting older is something all people share, an ultimate Recognition Factor for stories. With "Grousing" I was trying to examine a number of things about the process of aging by examining the relationship between two men of substantially different ages.

Maybe what I was looking for was an answer to the question, "How do we make this all work out?"

"Into the Twilight, Endlessly Grousing"

The old man sat across from me at the kitchen table in his cabin, polluting the air to lethal levels with a large illegal cigar someone had smuggled in to him and that his doctor had order him to stop smoking anyway.

"I know Doc ordered you to give up those cigars," I said. "Your smoking is bad for my health."

"That's because you're a pantywaist," he said. "This is a fine cigar, and if you had any taste at all, you'd appreciate its lovely aroma. Hemingway always brought me a couple of boxes from Cuba when he came up to hunt with me in Idaho. Now there was a man. They don't make them like Hem anymore, yourself being a case in point."

"I've heard all your Hemingway stories and don't believe a one of them," I said. "But they've improved over the years."

"Practice makes perfect," he said. "I ever tell you the time I outshot Hem on a grouse hunt? He wouldn't speak to me for two days afterwards, he was so mad. So then I let him beat me in arm wrestling, and then he was okay. I loved grouse hunting best of all. Almost best of all. Say, I got an idea. Let's go grouse hunting."

"You're too old and almost blind," I said kindly. "You can't see more than ten feet ahead of your nose. How are you going to shoot grouse?"

"You leave that to me," he said. "Now don't just stand there with your mouth hangin' open. Get me down one of my shotguns. The French twelve-gauge side-by-side will do."

"You gave that gun away years ago," I said.

"Well, that was a darn fool thing for me to do. Who'd I give it to?"

"Me."

"You! I would never give you a shotgun. You must have stole it."

"Nope, you gave it to me. It's mine now, and I'm keeping it. Anyway, it's much too fine a shotgun for a dirty old man like yourself. It's a gentleman hunter's gun. It's surprising any decent gun dealer would sell a fine instrument like that to an unsavory character like yourself."

"Interesting you should say that," he said. "I tried to be a gentleman hunter once, but it didn't take. Belonged to one of them elegant shooting clubs. Had to dress up like we was going to an afternoon tea rather than on a hunt. They had these pheasants penned up like a bunch of chickens and whenever we got ready for a hunt, one of the hired hands let a hundred or so of them loose and we'd go out and shoot them. The pheasants was tame, of course, so we'd practically have to kick them up in the air in order to get them to fly. So one day I said to the president of the club, I says 'Howard, this is a big nuisance, hunting pheasants this way. Why don't we just shoot them in the pens and be done with it? Save both the pheasants and us a lot of bother.' Well, that made Howard and some of the other gentlemen mad, and they booted me out of the club. So I quit the club right then and there. Figured it would teach them a good lesson."

"Served them right," I said.

"I thought so. Now stop standin' around jawing at me. If we're gonna go grouse hunting, we got to get to it. Fetch me the little Brit twenty-gauge."

I went to find the twenty-gauge. It was as fine a gun as I'd ever seen. The Old Man had been rich once, his guns now the only evidence of that former wealth. I figured he'd never worked. He was not the sort of man who would waste much effort on becoming rich. It had been a long time since he'd outlived his wealth, along with all his friends and enemies. "Mostly I did it to spite my enemies," he'd say, "but it got my friends, too."

He was very old now, ninety at least, maybe even a hundred; it was hard to tell, because he lied about everything, particularly his age. He was one of those peculiar old men who somehow managed to spend their entire lives enjoying themselves. He'd done just about everything there is to do, and what he hadn't done, he simply lied and claimed to have done that too. He was a very irritating old man, and I couldn't understand why I put up with him. I handed him the gun.

"Good," the Old Man said. "I was worried that you might have stole this one too."

"Just an oversight," I said. "I'll come back and get it some night when you're asleep."

"Ha!" he said. "That will take some doing. I ain't slept in twenty years. Now, here's my idea. We'll go out to that good grouse woods behind Jake Gregory's farm and you can flush some birds towards me, and I'll snap shoot them as they pass through my field of vision."

"Can't," I said. "Jake Gregory's woods is now a golf course."

"A golf course! They turned a good grouse woods into a golf course? I hate golfs. Well, we can go out there anyway, and you can flush some golfs towards me. How about that?"

"I don't think so."

"I know. We can go out to the mountain where Rancid Crabtree used to live and—"

"A shopping mall."

"A shopping mall! Good gosh a-mighty, what's a shopping mall doing way out in the country?"

"It's not way out in the country anymore. It's in town."

"They moved the mountain into town?"

"No. They moved the town out to the mountain. They've got condos all over the mountain."

"Condos? They good to eat?"

"Kind of tough and not much flavor. Taste a lot like golfs."

"Hunh! I don't like shoot-in' stuff that ain't fit to eat. Unless, of course it gets to be a nuisance. Let that be a lesson to you. Ain't there any good grouse woods about no more?"

"I know a couple of spots. But I like to keep them a secret. I show them to you, you'll be sneaking out there and shooting all my grouse."

"You bet. Now stop your yapping at me and let's go."

"Oh, all right." I said. "While you're walking out to the car, I'm going to have another cup of coffee or two and maybe read the newspaper. So you better get started."

"I've been started for the past five minutes. Shows how observant you are!"

I drove the Old Man over to my house and managed to kill a little time there while my wife, Bun, babied him and fed him some sponge cake with huckleberry sauce and whipped cream. She doesn't permit me to have whipped cream, a good indication of how much she prefers the Old Man.

I got my own gun and a vest full of shells, and considered whether to take the dog's shock collar. The collar works wonders for instilling obedience, but I wasn't sure how it would affect his pacemaker.

I finally extracted the Old Man from the fawning attention of Bun and inserted him back into the car.

"That's a fine woman," he said, licking the remnants of the whipped cream from his mustache. "She married?"

"You know she is," I said. "To me."

"You! What a waste!"

I drove out to one of my secret grouse woods and put the Old Man on a stand well out of range of my car. He sat down on a stump with a gun across his lap and a dead cigar clamped between his teeth.

"This is good grouse woods," he said. "It's a little blurry but it smell's right. You're too ornery to find me a clear grouse woods, but at least you found one that smells right. It sounds okay, too."

"Good," I said. "I'm going to circle around through the woods and see if I can flush some grouse towards you. Don't shoot anybody."

"I'm glad that you mentioned that. Otherwise, I wouldn't have known. If a golf comes by, I might try for it, though. How much lead on a golf?"

"A couple of feet if it's driving a cart flat out. If it's walking or running, you can pretty much hold right on. But there's a big fine if you shoot one."

I strolled off through the woods, enjoying it, feeling the press of birch leaves under my boots, listening to the rustle of small wild lives dart unseen for cover, smelling all the pungent smells of a grouse woods in late fall. I shot my first grouse in this same woods when I was about twelve, an amazing shot that would have been even more amazing if the grouse had been flying, instead of sitting on a limb. I was hunting all alone, the hand-me-down twelve-gauge shotgun big as a howitzer, and both barrels had gone off simultaneously and knocked me flat on my back, skinned up my trigger finger, and bloodied my nose. I thought the gun had exploded and was glad to still be alive, but it had shot true and killed the grouse stone dead. My mother was enormously pleased with the grouse, marveling that her son had brought home wild game. She cooked it in a gravy to pour over rice, and that one grouse could have fed twenty people, with some left over for the dog. I forgot to mention to anyone that the grouse had been sitting on a limb, but a kid can't be expected to remember everything.

I walked all the way through the woods and came out near a road on the other side, and by then I had three grouse, enough for my mother to have fed an army. All three shots were amazing, all wing shots too, with the grouse *burring* off through the trees, but none so amazing as the shot that took the first grouse fifty years ago. Did I say fifty? Surely I meant twenty. Yes, it couldn't possibly have been more than twenty years ago.

"How'd you do?" the Old Man asked me. "I heard a dozen shots. Even you must have got something with a dozen shots."

"Three grouse," I said. "How about you?"

"I did fine," he said. "None for none. It was a good hunt. This is a great grouse woods. By the way, what does that sign say over there? I been thinking about walking over there so I could read it, but then I figured I might not make it back before dark."

"That sign? Oh it just said, 'Private Property. No Hunting.'"

"Is that all?" the Old Man said. "I thought it might be something important."

On the way back to town, the Old Man mentioned that he'd gotten hungry from all his exertion. "Let's stop and get a bite at Gert's Gas 'N' Grub."

Gert herself came out to visit with us, and all the waitresses gathered around and made a big fuss over the Old Man, and he ate it all up, along with a chicken-fried steak and hash browns with gravy poured over them. He joked with the waitress and tried to pinch Gert on the behind, but she was too quick for him, as was almost everyone. Then a couple of the local boys joined in the festivities, and after a while one of them asked what we'd been up to.

"Grouse hunting," the Old Man said.

"Get any?" Red Barnes asked.

"I only got three," the Old Man said. "The boy here, he didn't get none. Did a lot of shooting though, so he had some fun. It was a good hunt."

"Well, I guess your eyes are still plenty sharp then," Gert said.

"Yep," the Old Man said. "Mighty sharp for a man my age — thirty-nine and some. Well, we best be going. Pay the bill boy, and leave the girls a big tip."

We didn't get back to the Old Man's cabin until after dark and he was pretty well tuckered out, although still smiling over all the attention heaped on him by the girls at Gert's. "I guess I still got it," he said.

"Yeah, right," I said. "It's just that you've got so old the women know you're harmless. First you get harmless, then you get lovable. That's the way it works with women."

"You're just jealous," he said.

I helped him to his cabin and was about to close the door behind him when I suddenly remembered. "Wait a minute," I said. "You left your gun in the car. I'll go get it."

"Naw," he said. "Keep it. Save us both the trouble of you stealing it from me later. That was a fine grouse woods. Mighty fine. I'd thank you for taking me there, but it'd just give you a big head."

I drove on home, happy in a way about the gift of the gun, but also not so happy. When you get right down to it, a gun is only a gun. I was glad it had been a good hunt though, and I was even more glad that I had lied about the sign next to the grouse woods. What it actually said was, "Future Site of the New Grouse Haven Golf Course and Condos!"

Newton: *Pat, do I catch a hint of Hemingway in the narration of "The Boy?"*

I suspect you do, Newton. I am a great fan of Hemingway and have learned a great deal about writing from studying his short stories, although it probably doesn't show up much in my humor pieces. Hem is quite easy to imitate. Too bad it isn't as easy to write short stories as well as he did. For some reason, I have found that in adopting the Hemingway voice, or my version of it, the voice itself will lead me into a story. Once I'm into the story, the voice tends to fade away, as I think happens here. As I've probably mentioned elsewhere, I'm a great believer in imitation of writer's voices you particularly like, especially for getting started on a piece of writing.

"The Boy"

Sometimes I'd take the boy fishing. He was not my boy but somebody else's, and that was good, his appetite and the cost of food being what they were. Mostly, I used him to hold down the bow of my canoe, instead of the bags of lead shot I usually employed for that purpose. He was smarter than the lead shot but not so much that you would notice.

"I wonder what causes the tides," he said once.

"The moon," I told him.

"The moon!" he cried, doubling over with laughter. "You expect me to believe that? You must think I'm stupid!"

I treated myself to a thoughtful pause.

"The earth is round," I said.

"So?" he said. "Everybody knows that."

"Just checking," I said.

The boy was about sixteen that year, the year I used him for lead shot. Whenever he ran out of money, which was often, he would come over to my cabin on the river and work for me. Mostly I would have him dig holes in the ground. When you own a cabin on a river, you always have need for lots of holes in the ground. I enjoyed listening to him complain about the pay, because then I knew I wasn't paying him too much. I prefer to err on the side of not enough, because it is wrong to spoil youngsters by paying them too much.

Whenever he complained about the pay, I would tell him about my first job. I was fourteen and worked for a farmer all one summer digging holes in the ground. The farmer was so cruel and sadistic that he had probably once been a commandant in charge of a slave labor camp. But I was the only one who suspected his previous employment. Everyone else thought he was a fair and decent and good-hearted man. But they didn't dig holes for him.

"Vork! Vork!" the farmer would scream at me.

About once a week I would get mad and resign my position. Then the farmer would come and tell my mother what a fine worker I was and that he wanted me to dig more holes. He told her that my work habits had improved greatly under his supervision, and now my pace was such that he could often detect movement with the naked eye. So Mom would make me go back to digging holes.

"Vork! Vork!" the farmer would scream.

By the end of summer, I hadn't earned quite enough money to buy my first deer rifle. The farmer gave me a bonus to make up the difference! I was astounded. Furthermore, I became the only person he would let hunt deer on his property, because I had been such a good and loyal worker and also because there were no deer there.

"So," I said to the boy, "do you see the moral to this story?"

"No," he said. "It's a boring story and I don't want to hear it ever again."

"Vork! Vork!" I shouted at him.

Sometimes, when the fishing was good, I would go out in the canoe almost every morning. I would get up very early and rush down to the river still buttoning my shirt, but the boy would be there already, waiting. I suspected he slept in the canoe, just so I couldn't slip away without him. We would paddle off to fish the channels that flowed between the islands where the river merged with the lake. As we paddled along we would exchange our theories about the purpose of human life. My theory was that the purpose of life was to perfect ourselves through learning and discipline in order to fulfill our cosmic responsibilities as part of the self-awareness of the universe. He thought the purpose of human life was for him to buy a car.

At the beginning of summer, the boy knew nothing about fishing, but by July he knew everything and had begun to advise me.

"That fly you're tying on is too big," he'd say. "Better go to a sixteen. And switch to a black gnat."

"How do you know all this?" I asked.

"It's easy, " he said. "I think like a fish."

"I can't argue with that," I said.

He enjoyed teasing me, because now he almost always caught more fish than I did. I would chuckle good-naturedly, smack the water just so with the paddle, and soak him to the skin.

The boy had a talent for getting on my nerves. I could remember how peaceful it had once been, when I was a solitary paddler, slipping quietly along the channels between the islands, doing everything just right, becoming one with nature and the mosquitoes and deerflies. But now the boy was always there, yakking, advising me on fishing technique, philosophizing about cars, complaining about the lunch I'd brought along and the pay he was getting for digging holes.

And then one morning he wasn't waiting for me at the canoe. He didn't come the next morning either. Or the following week. It was a relief. I was glad to be rid of him. Having nothing else to do, I asked around about him the next time I was in town. Most folks had no idea who he was, but the lady who runs the grocery said she thought he lived out on such-and-such road. Still having nothing else to do, I drove out the road and found an ancient mobile home approaching terminal depreciation under some scraggly pines. No one was home. A man stood watching me over a nearby fence.

"They's gone," he said. "Just packed up and left one day. Headed for Oklahoma. I'm from Oklahoma myself."

"Oklahoma," I said. "Any fishing there?"

"Good fishin'."

"I'm glad to hear it."

I went out fishing the next morning but it wasn't the same. A boy works a whole lot better than bags of lead shot for holding down the bow of a canoe, no question about it.

About a week later, another boy showed up at my cabin, apparently having heard I was short a boy. He was a redheaded kid with glasses that kept slipping down his freckled nose.

"I hear you got some work here," he said.

"I do," I said.

"What's the pay?"

I told him. He managed to stifle any hint of elation.

"What's the work?"

"I got all these holes I need filled up."

"I guess I can do that." He watched me for a moment, pushing his glasses back up his freckled nose. "What you doin' there to your canoe?"

"Nothing much," I said. "Just removing some bags of lead shot from the bow."

Commentary

Because "Grousing" and "Boy" have certain similarities, I thought I would comment on them as a matched pair. Each story has a bit more emotional depth than my typical humor piece in which the main purpose is to develop a comic idea and get a laugh, or at least a smile, from the reader. Without losing the humor, I wanted to suggest something about the way men relate to each other. The stories also express some of my thoughts about age and change and environment and the nature of life and so on, but never to the degree that they intrude upon the humor of the story. Or so I hope.

In both, "Boy" and "Grousing," the humor arises out of what appears on the surface to be an antagonistic relationship between the two main characters, between the narrator and a young boy in "Boy," and between the narrator and an old man in "Grousing."

The narrator in both stories expresses himself with a certain gruffness or irritability toward the other character but the reader is allowed to see through this facade and detect almost the opposite kind of feelings. I like to think both of these stories are examples of being "obscure clearly."

There are, of course, many obvious differences between the two stories, but I didn't become aware of the similarities until long after both were written. In other words, I didn't think to myself, "I liked the way 'Grousing' turned out, so I think I'll write another story like it." I suppose I could sit down now and invent a similar story but it probably wouldn't be very good. It seems to me that the best stories—and also the worst!— are the stories where you push yourself into new and unexplored regions of your own mind and creativity.

I had no idea where either of these stories was going when I started to write it. A deadline was looming in each case, and so I sat down and wrote a single sentence that I suppose simply popped into my head. That sentence led to another sentence and that to a scene and so on, and soon I began to become aware of a story emerging from the few words on the computer screen. I also began to get a sense of where the story line wanted to go. Stories don't actually write themselves but in some cases there seems to be a certain collaboration between you and the story, with the story, as it progresses, opening up certain possibilities that you take advantage of and try to develop. That was the case with each of these stories. I was well into the middle of both of them without knowing how they were going to end, but I had a strong sense of movement and directions for each. With "Boy," I knew the bag of lead shot had to be part of the ending and it fell naturally into place. With "Grousing," the ending was a little more difficult. I knew I needed some sort of surprise there, and I believe that I went back and inserted the sign into the story so that it could show up again as the "surprise" ending, and also wrap up one of the themes running through the story. Actually, the sign was already in the story to indicate the Old Man's faulty eyesight and the slowness of his movements and also something about his personality. What I changed was the wording on the sign. Stories do not always develop as organic wholes and sometimes you have to go back and insert bits and pieces of information or scenes in order to give the story a sense of completion, something that says in effect, "Hey, this story just ended!" I am paid to be a humor writer, and so even if I write a story that may have deeper emotional elements in it than the usual humor piece, the humor still has to be there. One reason I particularly like "Grousing" and "Boy" is that the humor seems to arise naturally out of the personalities of the characters and out of their relationships.

Humorists I've Liked and Learned From

Humorists I've Liked and Learned From

George Ade

The Permanent Ade: The Living Writings of George Ade (1947)

I've read some of George Ade, and like him. He is a favorite of crossword puzzle authors, so you can see there is some value in having a last name of only three letters.

Woody Allen

Getting Even (1971)
Without Feathers (1975)
Side Effects (1980)

I like Woody's comic essays far better than his movies.

Dave Barry

Babies and Other Hazards of Sex (1993)

Dave Barry is amazing. Year after year he remains at the top of his game as the funniest newspaper humor columnist around and besides that seems to turn out another book every year.

Robert Benchley

My Ten Years in a Quandary and How They Grew (1939)
Chips Off the Old Benchley (1949)
The Benchley Roundup (1954)

Benchley dominated humor writing throughout the 30's and into the 40's. He may seem a bit dated but you can learn much from him.

Roy Blount

What Men Don't Tell Women (1984)

Camels Are Easy, Comedy's Hard (1991)

Roy Blount has long been one of my favorite authors. He has written some of the funniest stories in the English language.

Erma Bombeck

The Grass Is Always Greener over the Septic Tank (1976)

Motherhood, The Second Oldest Profession (1983)

All I Know about Animal Behavior I Learned in Loehmann's Dressing Room (1995)

Erma Bombeck has written some wonderful humor and a terrific amount of it. Unlike some newspaper humor columnists, her columns seem less dated because they are not so topical.

Art Buchwald

The Buchwald Stops Here (1978)

Buchwald has written some great stories and anyone interested in writing humor for newspapers should read him. Because his columns usually relate to political events of the day, the humor may be a little difficult to grasp without the historical background.

Garrison Keillor

Happy to Be Here (1982)

Lake Woebegone Days (1985)

Garrison Keillor's work seems written to be read aloud, which he does very well. It's interesting to read one of his stories and then listen to it read on tape. Unlike most authors, Keillor adds to his writing by reading it aloud. Most of the rest of us subtract.

Farley Mowat

The Dog Who Wouldn't Be (1957)

Farley Mowat, along with more serious work, has written some great comedy pieces. He has long been one of my favorites.

S.J. Perelman

The Best of S.J. Perelman (1947)

The Rising Gorge (1960)

S.J. Perelman is an acquired taste, but once you've acquired the taste you will love Perelman. His comedy is so rich and complex, however, it is hard to learn from, although he does have a few imitators out there.

Jean Shepherd

In God We Trust, All Others Pay Cash (1966)

Jean Shepherd may be the funniest writer I've ever read. He is best known for his movie *A Christmas Story*.

James Thurber

My Life and Hard Times (1933)

My World and Welcome to It (1942)

Alarms and Diversions (1957)

A Thurber Carnival (1962)

Thurber has come as close as any humorist in this country to achieving literary status, even though he himself seems to have thought he had been denied it. "The writer of short humor pieces," he wrote, "sits on the edge of the chair of literature." Or something close to that.

Calvin Trillin

Enough's Enough and Other Side Effects (1990)

Trillin is an interesting writer from whom much can be learned about the writing of humor.

Mark Twain

Roughing It (1872)

I've listed only one book by Twain, but you should read everything by him you can get your hands on. In my opinion, *Roughing It* is his funniest book by far.

E. B. White

One Man's Meat (1944)

The Second Tree from the Corner (1954)

The Points of My Compass (1962)

White has long been one of my favorite writers and I read something from the books listed here at least once a year and probably more often. His essays are not humor pieces as such, but an undercurrent of humor runs through everything he has written.

About the Author

Patrick McManus's last work of fiction was *Into the Twilight, Endlessly Grousing*. He has been an editor-at-large of *Outdoor Life* for the last two decades and is also a professor emeritus of Eastern Washington University.

more great books from
EWU PRESS

EWU
P·R·E·S·S

Title	ISBN	Author	Reg.	Special
The Talking Book of July PB	0-910055-35-1	Rick Alley	12.00	7.78
The Talking Book of July HC	0-910055-35-1	Rick Alley	23.00	14.92
Divorce Boxing PB	0-910055-43-2	D.C. Berry	14.00	9.08
Divorce Boxing HC	0-910055-43-2	D.C. Berry	24.00	15.57
The Words of Bernfrieda PB	0-910055-49-1	Gabriella Brooke	18.95	12.29
Hangar Talk	0-910055-40-8	Irv Broughton	35.00	22.70
I Remember the Fallen Trees PB	0-910055-45-9	Elizabeth Cook-Lynn	15.95	10.35
The Deathbed Playboy PB	0-910055-47-5	Philip Dacey	14.00	9.08
The Deathbed Playboy HC	0-910055-48-3	Philip Dacey	24.00	15.57
They Dream, They Cry, They Sing PB	0-910055-42-4	Perry Higman	16.00	10.38
They Dream, They Cry, They Sing HC	0-910055-41-6	Perry Higman	25.00	16.22
Memory and Heaven PB	0-910055-28-9	Christopher Howell	14.00	9.08
Memory and Heaven HC	0-910055-27-0	Christopher Howell	24.50	15.89
Out of the Channel PB	0-910055-53-X	John Keeble	14.00	9.08
Out of the Channel HC	0-910055-54-8	John Keeble	26.00	16.86
Picking and Choosing HC	0-910055-25-4	Carolyn Kizer	25.00	16.22
The Mother's Poems/ Gabriela Mistral	0-910055-29-7	Christiane Jacox Kyle	25.00	16.22
Hmong: History of a People HC	0-910055-24-6	Keith Quincy	27.50	17.48
The Fair and the Falls HC	0-910055-33-5	J. William T. Young	56.00	36.32

ORDER FORM

TITLE: Price:

_____

_____

_____

_____

_____

                          Total: _____

MASTERCARD OR VISA ACCEPTED
(PLEASE CIRCLE CARD TYPE)
CARD NO. _____
EXP. DATE _____
SIGNATURE _____

Make checks payable to:
EASTERN WASHINGTON
UNIVERSITY PRESS
MAIL STOP 1, 705 WEST 1ST AVE.
SPOKANE, WA 99201-3909
EWU
P·R·E·S·S   1-800-508-9095, Fax 509-623-4283

Name _____

Address _____

Phone _____